Dear Felix Diary Thingy,
Felix, in the Time of Confused

Copyright 2020 - Kathy LaFollett | All Rights Reserved

No part of this book may be reproduced without permission.
Contact author directly via FlockCall.com for reproduction permissions.

Seriously, just email me first.

Cover Art – Kathy LaFollett

ISBN - 9798687586450

Foreword by Kathy LaFollett

We did not plan Felix. We were there to buy parrot toys, food, and dog things that day. The universe allows us to think quietly amongst ourselves while it lays its rails down forcing our choices to change trajectory toward its requirements. There was a store closer. But we were out doing other Saturday things and stopped where the universe placed Felix two days before.

The universe is impatient. There is no time to waste, infinite as it is. We took ten steps into the store and there was Felix in a cage too small, perched facing backwards letting the world know it wasn't part of Felix's universal plans. He was waiting for us. We just didn't know it, yet.

We paused together to admire him. I noted his body language: full of stress. Cali opened the door of the cage and invited Felix out.

You know those romantic movies that switch to slow motion when the couple that walked right by each other during the first seventy minutes finally run into each other and realize they're a thing? That. I saw slow mo parrot step up on the hand of a slow mo dad on Saturday. Hence, why I call dad/Cali, SaturDADday.

Felix scrambled onto Cali's shoulder and claimed him. Mine. All this here, is mine. I laughed. Cali laughed. Felix was silent. Cali asked Felix to step up again and then offered Felix the opportunity to meet me on my waiting hand. He stepped with ease and confidence. I felt he understood how confused I was, and that he wanted to help.

That was 2011. We called him Franklin because the store owner said that was his name. It wasn't. The store owner said, "Franklin is on consignment because his previous owner got sick."

Felix came home and took over home without a word. He perched on his new cage, rods running the width on top. Bowls positioned on either side. In front of what would become, the Weirdo Neighborling Window. He perched relaxed with a talon of fury full of walnut. Eating.

His attention went around the room taking in all the work he had to do. He glanced at me, then Cali, then the dogs. So much confused. So little time. Where are the pistachios?

I spent three months calling him Franklin. He would correct me each morning with "Hello Felix!"

Three months he labored in words trying to teach me truths.

"Time to take a shower!"

"Hey Harry! Stop that over there!"

"Hello, Jim."

answering machine kicking in "Hello, you there, what? Okay." BEEP

He served a dozen good scenario sentences introducing all his life names. It was, "Felix wants some apple." That gave me pause. After three months. Yes, I am confused.

That night I put Felix to bed saying, "Night Felix. I love you."

Franklin was the guy that loved him first.

Felix was Felix. And the clouds parted revealing a parrot's intentions.

Felix's goal is training. Removing The Confused and placing knowledge in the gaping hole. Felix travels with me to kids camps, rescues, and shelters teaching the way of the parrot via the Way of the Grey. He inspired my first book; *The Art of the FlockCall: Creating your Successful Companion Parrot Lifestyle*.

He became a social media personality. He wrote a book. He ran for president in 2016 and wages again in 2020. Because removing The Confused and placing knowledge in the gaping hole is his calling.

Felix judges no one. He judges confused. Felix loves all, but The Confused itself. Felix represents the clearest view of contentment. Contented without The Confused.

And so we bring you this second book of The Felix. His thoughts and diary entries over the years. Notation Expositions are mine. Clarifying the moment in time. Chronological in presentation. Parrot in perspective. You can jump onto his Facebook page and find the day of these entries if you like. His memes will add a bit of color.

A parrot that has authored, traveled, delivered sermons of sense, ran for President in two consecutive races, and is a standing member of the Parrot Party for Liberation of the Confused. His words are sage, if not just a tad loud.

We love our Felix. We love sharing him with the world. We don't have a choice.

Yours, confused,
Felix's Mom

Editor's Note by Michelle Devon

Seven or eight years ago, I sat in my living room fighting back tears and wrapping my hand, dripping with blood, with a towel, wondering if I'd bitten off more than I could chew this time, with this, this, this… BIRD I had in my house. I knew the transition would be difficult from the only safe house he'd ever been in with people who loved him (his foster home) to my home full of strangers. He was a rescue from a bad situation, after all. I just never realized how physically painful it would be.

It was in this moment of deep despair that Jon, Memphis's foster dad, sent me a link to a post about cockatoos on Kathy LaFollett's Facebook page. I started laughing at the humor, and then started reading more that she wrote. Before long, I was crying tears of laughter and it wasn't long before I picked up my training treats and started in with Memphis again.

Kathy probably doesn't remember this but she suggested to me something I already knew well, but needed the gentle reminder: **words are powerful.** If Memphis bites every time we say 'step up', quit saying step up! The theory? He was likely punished or treated poorly in relation to those words, so find new words. What a simple concept. If he bites you for doing that, don't do that!

We started using, "Hop!" instead. To this day, we still say hop when we want him to step up and he does it. If we forget and slip in a "step up", he nips us to remind us we are doing it wrong. He's a harsh trainer.

Felix, Kathy's trainer, makes fun of her all the time, but I find she's not confused nearly as much as Felix says she is. She's helped my flock through so much, those little moments when you feel stressed and can't see the problem from the inside. Kathy has been there to see the problem through her unique eyes. I would say her spirit is a bird, but really, she's crazy about any animal. She feels the call of the wild from ducks to blue jays and crows and lizards not to mention furry things of all sizes. Her life is full of the fun chaos that makes it worth living and I am but a voyeur at her antics, like any of you.

My family got to meet Kathy in person at a speaking gig she did in Houston. She walked into the room with an octopus hat on her head. She acted like it wasn't there at first and just spoke to the group. One thing for sure, you weren't going to miss that octopus on her head. To this day, when Memphis or one of our other flock members (we have five feathered flock in all) transitions slowly and there's something new in the room or on our bodies (jewelry, hat, glasses, etc.), we still say, "But you have an octopus on your head!"

And it's gems like that where Kathy can take what makes perfect sense to the bird and make it make sense to the human in the equation too. Every time I read Felix, I learn something more about my birds. Every time I read Kathy, I learn something more about life.

That's why it is such an honor to be asked to write this foreword for a book I know is going to help so many people and flocks. Laughter, true humor, is the only way to go through life without cracking up and Kathy and her flock brings plenty for you in this compilation of years' worth of anecdotes, jokes, guffaws, mistakes, and goof ups. But you're also going to find some poignant moments to carry you through, those moments that touch your heart and maybe make you tear up a little when you read them.

Because that's Kathy: humor and poignancy, laughter and love, flock and friend.

Thank you for the friendship and all of the above, Kathy. Congratulations on another fantastic book.

Michelle Devon
Author, Feathered Flock Mom
Professional Dreamer....

A Trainer's Foreword by Memphis Cockatoo

I, Memphis the Cockatoo, remember all that mom says about the finger biting. It's not like that though. I didn't draw THAT much blood in the beginning, and she only had to go the 'mergent room one time for a broken finger. The other time she went it was just a fracture. It's not my fault she didn't understand that 'step up' makes me crazy, right?

But that was a long time ago and then Mom found Felix. That's when I remember everything getting better for our flock. Mom started to make sense, where before she was just really confused. She started asking me to do things the right way and so I had no choice but to stop biting. It's in the bird handbook we all have that when trainees behave properly, we are not allowed to bite them.

Now, I know there are some birds out there who were never lucky enough to get to be with parronts who love them so no one gave them the bird handbook. That's why Felix's book here is so important. It takes the place of the bird handbook for those of us who didn't get adopted by good people from the start.

My brother Hatch and I, along with Conner, Bob and Woz (our other flock members), all work together to train mom in the right ways to integrate a feathered flock with a human household. Mom is learning her training really well.

Kathy and Felix are big parts of that training with mom. They help with the humans in the equation to try to translate the bird vocabulary for us so we can all communicate better. Communication is the key for being a happy flock together.

That, to me, Memphis the Cockatoo, is what this book is ultimately about: communication. Communication between you and your flock, Kathy and her flock, mom and her flock, Mom and Kathy, Kathy and her readers, and and and, wow, lots of communications going on. That just goes to show how important all this communication stuff is. It leads to understanding, empathy, corporation, family and flock dynamics.

If not for Felix training his mom, my mom would be a lot more confused and might have fewer fingers than she does now. And then I wouldn't be able to cuddle with her the way I love to snuggle at night when it's quiet. But don't tell her I enjoy that. I need her to think I do it for her benefit. You've got to keep these trainees in line, you know.

I'll tell you a secret if you promise not to tell Kathy or mom: I love my flock now and I love my mom and I wouldn't trade what I have now for anything. That's why I say, "Hello!" and "Hop!" so often because it makes mom so happy. There's something to be said for having a happy trainee.

So thank you, Fee and of course Kathy for showing mom the light. I don't know what we'd do without you. You're rock stars in the Memphis book of rock stars!

Memphis the Cockatoo

April 20th, 2012

Your understanding and our story starts and ends with the thoughts of a parrot.

The Story by Felix

After 19 1/2 years with Harry, I found myself in a cage alone. Harry wasn't acting right. He was always tired, and he sometimes forgot to feed me. So one day, when Harry wasn't thinking about me, they showed up. They called him dad and they called me bird. And they put me in a cage I didn't know and took me to a place I didn't know and left me with people I did not know.

But I knew I didn't like any of it. This place was loud. My home with Harry wasn't loud. This place had loud people and unhappy animals making loud sounds. My home with Harry didn't have other people or unhappy animals. Harry was a good guy. This place smelled wrong, and sounded wrong and all anybody asked was "how much?" and "does he talk?" Confused questions are annoying. Those are the wrong questions! I have questions, but no one is listening to me. I now have a bowl full of seeds and a water bowl full of water from a tap. It's wrong. This is all wrong and I am on my last nerve endings.

So there I am in a cage I don't know. Stuck between two birds in cages they don't seem to know either. I don't know what is going to happen. And we are stuck in front of a door that is opening and closing a lot and it is cold. Annoying. Talk to the buttfeather. I give everybody my back. I refuse to turn around.

The cockatoo to my right wing is naked and jumping up and down every time somebody looks at him.

I tell him to ignore all these people and their faces and their yells and their confused questions, and their fingers poking in the cage. But he won't listen. The bird to my left wing is old. He's an old Military Macaw. I can tell he's been through all this before. He barely looks at me or any birdy else.

And so it goes all day. My cage is so short I just see belts and bellies and purses and hands. I can't see faces to tell who is what and what they want. I refuse to look up. I won't. Neither will the cockatoo or the macaw. We all decide not to look. Noise, hands, cold. I hate this ridiculous.

And so the first day of people poking inside my wrong cage, and people upsetting cockatoo that won't listen to me, and people talking to macaw that won't listen to them, ends. This is ridiculous on my last nerve endings. I turn my back to it all. I do not know what is going to happen.

It's dark, it's bedtime. Where's my real cage? Where's my real dinner? Where's my real roost? Where is Harry? The lights go out. We are alone except the other animals. No one said good night. No one said goodbye. No one said see you later. They just left us. I do not know what is going to happen. I can't sleep much. It's not dark. There are lights flashing from cars outside on the fast moving street. The cockatoo is rocking a lot. He can't perch still. I don't blame him though.

I must have fallen asleep because I woke up to hands in the cage. Hands putting more seeds in my dish. I'm hungry, but I'm not eating that. I can't eat any of that. And so the day goes like the day before. People, cold, loud, people poking my cage, the cockatoo jumping. I turn my back to it all. And then it gets worse.

SO many people start coming in with dogs on leashes I can't see anywhere.

My cage is blocked by so many people and dogs! Dogs sniffing the cage I hate and looking at me with doghead eyes. I'm stuck! I'm trapped. It's louder, it's faster, it smells worse and dogheads are everywhere. The people and dogheads make a line out the door and the door stays open. We are all cold now, and we can't get warm because of the line of people and dogheads. Ridiculous! I turn my back on all of this and close my eyes. I don't remember making a wish, but I suppose I must have, because when I opened my eyes I heard a voice behind me.

"Hey buddy, what's your name?" Now that was a nice voice, with a proper question! I didn't turn around, I didn't want him to leave. He didn't sound like Harry, but he sounded nice like Harry.

"It's okay, I won't leave just yet. You must really hate it here. It's so cold!" And so this voice kept saying really nice things and never asked questions. He just said things I was thinking and what I worried about, which was nice. I wasn't alone. I was going to turn around and take the chance of this nice guy disappearing when another voice showed up.

"Aw!" A girl voice. I knew that much. "What's his name? He has his back to you, he seems upset."

The nice not Harry voice answered her. "Poor guy, he is really upset. Let me talk with him a while."

"Of course!" she said. "I'll stay with you, let's move these people away from his cage. This is ridiculous."

I turned around to find mom and dad making people move AWAY! They knew it was all ridiculous! I needed to rescue them.

I knew he was my new dad, I knew that after he asked my name. And since they came as a pair, well that's a 2fer deal! So mom stood in front of the cage I hated and told people I was theirs and they needed to stand somewhere else. And I talked to my new dad. He is very good at listening.

Dad opened the cage I hated and asked if I wanted to step up. How polite. Yes, yes I would! So I perched on dad's warm hand and we talked some more. Mom kept telling people to stand somewhere else with their dogs. She is very good at doghead controls.

I asked to step on mom. Sometimes you have to take chances to get what you need. So I stuck my foot right out and up and waited for her to get the gist. She did pretty quick, too! So I perched on mom's warm hand and we talked. Dad left to talk to some guy, I saw him talking to that guy pointing at me and the cage I hate. Some boy walked up to mom while I was watching dad, and tried to get me. I ran up to mom's shoulder and looked down at him. That boy said, "Can I hold that bird?"

Mom said, "This is my companion parrot. No, you can't touch him." I DID know what was going to happen!

Dad came back and said, "Ready to go home Franklin?" My name isn't Franklin. That guy he talked to made that up. But that's okay. I can train mom and dad at home.

So here is The Felix, sitting in his house and ready to do something with a new flock family. Of course I train them every day.

And mom and I decided we better get busy and help others right away!

Because I am not the only parrot in the world that needs understanding. Because to understand companion parrots, you have to think like a companion parrot. And to think like a companion parrot, it's easier to learn by watching somebody else do it. So mom is a really good sport about all this and we work together to show any one that wants to know, what a parrot really thinks and what a parrot really needs. And it's way easier to learn this laughing while you learn it.

There was always a plan. My plan was to go home with mom and dad. Her plan is to show just how much companion parrots really think, appreciate, eat, sleep, act, need, laugh, play, joke and need a flock. Now you know the story and the plan.

This first day with mom and dad is exhilarating!

April 21st, 2012

A good night's sleep resets a parrot in a good way.

They both seem sincere in their efforts. Yesterday was overdone. All the introductions and tours. Who introduces a Felix to a window? My new cage is obvious, tree stand and table and stand and...she seems intent on overdoing. Dinner was delicious! Pistachios and a Felix Snack Attack Table next to dad's chair for attacking snacks. Mom gets excited overdoing offerings. Which is fine, except for asking if I want warm teas every time I look up. I have to look up a lot so I have to train her to ask when I do something else. Maybe the Eye of Regret, I will worry about that later.

Yes, new mom is going to need the work.

Bedtime went better than expected. I have my own room, and roost.

At bedtime, they stood there with me looking at it and talking about whether it is the right cage, should I be covered, is this what I want. Back and forth and back and forth they talked to each other about all the bedroom needs of Felix. Which is fine. My needs are what they need to be talking about. They said good night Franklin, and dad petted me and then I stepped up for mom; she tried so hard during the day so, you know, she probably needed that. She got all clingy and started talking about wanting to scratch my head. GAH!

I stepped into my new bedroom cage and realized...oh! it is the same cage as at the store they rescued me from, but wait, they fixed it to be right. A very feets comfy perch for sleeping and I do appreciate the covers. A bird needs some shut eyes and privacies. And a towel of comfortables is on my cage floor in case I need to take a walk about. My talons of fury will appreciate the comfortables.

The first day and night went pretty good. I can see the training to come, but it was a good day.

This morning is interesting. Which is to say that I am interested in how she is going to fix all this confused.

June 10th, 2013

In the beginning Felix felt it imperative to instruct all Trainees on food: the use, taste, and necessary guidelines for their Trainers. The low blood sugars were heavy on his mind.

Sometimes I don't like food because it's shaped wrong. I can't eat broccoli if it's not upside down. I can't eat the bitty green balls first. I can't eat the celery if it is not chopped in the U shape. The U's fit my Talons of Fury. Just because I don't like it, doesn't mean I won't like it if you fix the shape.

Try this at home with your Personal Trainer immediatlies! What else are you going to do with all those vega-tables? Throw them on the dogheads?

Of the course not, that is our job.

July 11th, 2013

Transportation and logistics were a big deal for Felix as well. Even in the early days, we could see a Presidential lean in the personality of Felix. He was here to do big things for all parrots, big or small.

I have decided I will be using the Mom Taxi for transport. Flying is annoying. If I fly, dactyls[1] show up where I was, getting into the Felix businesses. Worse than that annoying, someone is already there where I was going! Or worse than the worst, someone follows me.

Flying is annoying. Mom Taxi is better because no one knows where mom is going or why. Not even mom. That fixes followers and already there-ers.

July 15th, 2013

Mom made foot toys today. She calls them Paper Burritos[2]. I call them Thingys I must murder immediatelies. Same thing really.

---

[1] Dactyl, Felix's name for Butters and Snickers, his blue and gold and scarlet macaws, respectively. Felix's flock is fully flighted. Mobility creates air traffic control needs.

[2] Paper Burrito is a foot toy created from half a paper towel roll stuffed full with newspaper, confetti, and any shreddable papers. (Newsprint ink and paper towel rolls glue is not a threat. Please visit *flockcall.com* for an article explaining inks and glues in the era of recyclable and renewable materials.) The Felix Flock love a good paper burrito.

She is so easy to entertains. There she is giggling watching the Felix murder the Paper Burrito with my Talons of Fury. Sometimes she gets so excited about these thingys I have to drop them and walk away. She gets over the stimulation. Moms are like that.

July 16th, 2013

Low Blood Sugars and concern for his mother's embarrassment over the awkward moments she created became a focus during that summer. His Personal Trainer[3] work was secure in her confused.

My face is empty. My foods bowl is empty. This is pretty awkward for mom. Can you imagine how embarrassing not feeding The Felix right after breakfast is? She is probably hiding in the closet right the now. She's probably in the closet saying, "I can't believe I didn't feed The Felix his after breakfast, before lunch, snack attacks! I am so shambled!"

That's probably why my foods bowl and my face are empty. Mom is in the closet suffering the mortificationings.

She better get over it. I can feel the low blood sugars creeping up my buttfeathers.

July 22nd, 2013

There was a moment in time when Felix felt compelled to enter the world of interior design and Feng Shui, (as it pertained to his personal space), (when mom was around), (bringing things).

---

[3] Personal Trainer, a term for all parrots training their humans. Felix wrote about this subject in his bestselling book, *"Directions for the Confused; How to Think Like a Parrot"*. His tome made the Number One selling book on Amazon on its release date.

Obviouslies mom has decided that The Felix wall is the museums of art that I don't want to look at. She tried to put a painting of two rabbits eating lettuce on my wall. I can't eat around that.

She tried to put a drawing of two parrots sitting on a digest perch. I have two dactyls for the reals, why am I looking at that drawing?

Then she said, "Oh look Felix! It's a mirror. Very pretty, and you can see yourself and talk to yourself whenever you want!"

She is off her rocker chair. Why would I talk to myself? I already know what I am thinking.

I told Butters Dactyl to go ahead and pull all that off The Felix walls. Now she is sitting on a table looking in the mirror talking to herself.

I am exhausted.

August 1st, 2013

The beats for my feets are groovy today. David the Bowie is rocking and the rollering. I was minding my own businesses dancing the beats and then mom thinks alone, and starts dancing with The Felix.

She's either dancing or she's got the fleas. If she has the fleas, they are not on the beats at all. She and her fleas are doing all that in front of my Weirdo Neighborling Window!

If he sees her, he will think WE are weirdo.

We are not.

But mom has fleas that can't dance. That's more annoying than weirdo. I will have to come up with a flea fix.

August 2nd, 2013

Today I got a new tree stand thingy. Mom put a Felix Towel on it to make the Felix Tree Tent Stand Thingy. And a bowl for snack attacks. And a phonesbook inside the tent to explode. I'm not saying she is not confused. But I am going to admit this is cereally good stuffings here.

I got on my new tree stand and there are wheels under there! She pushed me around.

"Felix this is your new tree stand taxi! I can take you anywhere you want. Just point your face to where you want to go."

My Felix Tree Tent Taxi Stand Thingy has power steering!

August 7th, 2013

I am going to make a snack attack calendar for mom. She expected me to eat yesterday's snack today. I ate those yesterday's. I can't eat yesterdays today. I might eat yesterday's tomorrow, but probably not.

I could eat yesterday's next week. But not the day after tomorrow.

Day after tomorrow is SaturDADday. Pancakes for The Felix made by dad. Which if anyone would ask, I will eat every day.

But no one is asking The Felix about this important snack attack matter.

August 8th, 2012

Mom did it again. She rescued another cockatiel to add to her Horde[4] already here being annoying.

"Oh look, Felix! This is Winston! He needed a home, and since Stella needed a friend I asked him to live with us! Isn't he adorable with his white face?"

Excuse the me, I am adorable with a white face. You don't need two of this adorable. Alsotoo, how many cockatielers do you need to rescue? How big is your Horde going to get with you helping?

I do not have the time for this. I am training the already here Horde, the dactyls[5] and the Kirby Lurker[6]!

I am still training her, obviouslies.

August 26th, 2013

Mom and dad got the dactyls a giant tree stand. It is taller than dad. The branches fit my feets. This tree thingy is perfect! I have decided it is mine.

The tree thingy foods bowls are perfect! There's Felix foods in them! They fit my face. Those are now mine, alsotoo. There is way too many hilarious and delicious in this giant tree stand thingy for dactyls.

---

[4] Horde is the term referring to the flock of cockatiels living with Felix. A flock of cockatiels flying in a house does resemble a horde of barbarians.
[5] Dactyl, Felix's two macaws, Butters and Snickers.
[6] Kirby Luker is an Indian Ringneck Parakeet that lives without a cage. He is free to go anywhere in the Felix house. He and Felix get along quite well. Lurker is a term used to describe his natural tendency to life.

September 6th, 2013

Breakfast was delicious today. I got the Smashed Hash Tatters with the chopped broccolis that didn't touch the slicered apples. I ate the seconds on the Smashed Hash Tatters.

Life is too short to not eat the second Smashed Hash Tatters.

September 13th, 2013

Mom is painting pictures on the walls. All over the places. There are trees, and fish, and water, and sky, and the manatee, which looks like a walrus with no teeth if you ask me. And a giant sea turtle swimming.

I have to help her keep her painter brushes in the line. When they roll around on the floor I throw them to teach them the lessonings of not rolling around. Then mom runs to her paint brusher to finish the lesson.

I have to throw a lot of paint brushes. She didn't buy the smartest paint brushes. She should have taken The Felix to buy the smart paint brushes. But, no one asked The Felix to help make sure smart brushes came home in the bag from the store with the smart chalk and ruler that do not roll anywhere. How awkward was every thing in that bag?

September 17th, 2013

TSUNAMI!! My feathers are soggy stuck. I was going to take the water bowl bath, if someone had asked The Felix. But no, dad just said, "Let's take the showerings Felix!"

Next thing I know; TSUNAMI!!! Before breakfast. I can't eat with soggy stuck feathers.

Now I am sitting with stuck soggy feathers eating breakfast, dripping in my foods bowls. How annoying. I won't even look at mom until lunch.

September 19th, 2013

Today is Talk like a Pirate Day!

I be Capt'n Jack Felix! I have the fist full of the booty snacks! I pirated this here loot from that swab, Kirby.

What's this? Belay that talk salty'ma!

For ye sound like ye have a head cold. Aye! Ye sound ridiculous! Leave the pirate'n to Capt'n Jack Felix! YarGAR!!!

I need more booty, alsotoo.

September 25th, 2013

Today is the hot mess. Snickers Dactyl jumped on my cage and stole my snacks. He just splatted on my cage, opened my snack attack foods bowl and stole my snacks! And not the snacks that I don't want, either!

Splatting dactyls are annoying.

September 30th, 2013

Dad made the Bee Bee Que chicken, corncob corns and stuffed up pastas for dinner. It is called the Dad's Football Game Feastings.

Then the Bucs did something in the football game and dad ran over to the TV to yell at it.

Why he is yelling at the TV I don't know. TV didn't do anything. Alsotoo, I did not know the TV's name is Schiano.

"WHAT ARE YOU DOING SCHIANO!?!?!?"

Since dad is busy yelling at Shiano TV, I ate his feast. Never let a feast get cold.

Even if your TV, Schiano, doesn't know what it is doing.

October 23rd, 2013

Butters Dactyl chomped mom's monitor thingy. I don't know why this computer monitor is such the big important deal any theway. She has two.

When one of my foods bowls are empty I go to the other one. And if that foods bowl is empty, I go to the other, other one. Wait. Maybe that is her problem.

She better get lots of the monitors and put them all over the place. She should ask The Felix for advice.

October 28th, 2013

It seems The Horde is training mom. This is good. One less thing for me to do today.

December 2nd, 2013

'Tis the seasonings for annoying. The Horde pooped on my tent. What am I supposed to do with that? I can't look at any of that. I'm not going in there. This is the problem with Hordes. There are lots of them. And when one poops every thebody else poops and then what I am going to do? My tent is covered in the poop mines!

Mom says, "Don't worry Felix, I will get another towel in a minute."

In a minute! In a minute could get horde poop on my Talons of Fury and then what!? GAH! I can't move.

I...I think I lost a butt feather.

December 6th, 2013

"Felix, let's have some fun!"

"Okay! Give me pistachios."

"No. I have a better fun surprise. Let's go for a ride. You love riding in the truck."

And this was where mom became a traitor. Yes, I like the big red trucker. I like riding to places to train childrens. Mostly because did you know, children are not confused. Grown ups are. If I can catch children before they get all grown uppy, the confused has no chances. So, yes, if the big red trucker is heading to children to train. I love riding in the truck.

But that is not what traitor mom had in the brain. She points the big red trucker to the doctor. Traitor.

First, Dr. NoseItAll burritos The Felix in a smelly not my towel, towel. A Felix Burrito? Really? Are you Cereal?!?

Then she points lights up my nose holes, in my eye balls, and up my you know whats.

"Oh Felix you look great!"

Of the course I look great! I am the Felix! Stop looking up my butt.

Then she grabs my Talons of Fury and wiggles them. And my wings and looks at them. And my Beak of Dismantling and kisses it! KISSES MY BEAK OF DISMANTLING!

What a weirdo.

Then she puts me on the thingy that says Felix is a perfect 452 grams of perfect. No surprises here.

Then she says, "Felix you look great!"

I drove all the way over here thinking I was going there for THIS?

Then mom says, "Thank you, doctor." Because obviouslies she enjoyed the show. Traitor.

Here we are at home again. I will not look at mom until dinner. Or maybe before dinner snack. Or the after lunch before dinner snack attack of delicious. What time is it any theway? I am discomburberated.

December 23rd, 2013

Felix enjoys poems and prose. Seasonally he'll take That Guy's Pen[7] in talon and write to his muse, Santa Claus. Felix has never been on Santa's naughty list.

T'was the night before the Christmas,
And all through the tent,
<u>Not a dactyl was stirring w</u>ith ridiculous intent.

---
[7] Any pen found in the house that Felix considers usable for his plans, planning, or throwing.

The Horde called no meeting to do nothing at all,
While Kirby Lurker was not busy
Changing in the Kirby Shredder down the hall.

I in my tree stand thingy, and dad in his chair,
Mom was confused, but I didn't care.

It's quiet, and peaceful, and Christmasy right!
But what? What happened? That's just a fright!

Up with a start, what was that noise!?!
Two dogheads, stealing dactyl squeaky toys!

Dactyls are up! Kirby is here!
The Horde called a meeting!
This is not Felix Christmas Cheer!

Dogheads should be outside under the boat.
I could probably train mom to dig a moat.

It's all too ridiculous, no one is trained!
Merry Felix Christmas! I am already drained.

December 31st, 2013

Mom says she is revolving to work smarter and not harder.
That is hard to believe.

She should revolve to pay attentions to training more. She would be less confused and more trained if she revolved her attentions.

Someone needs to revolve to bring me more appreciations. That would be a good revolution.

Dactyls need to revolve not to be so dactyly. See all that dactyly dactyl over there? So Ridiculous.

Dad should revolve to make more pancakes. I am ready for a pancake revolution!

January 4th, 2014

Good the news!

I finalies trained Butters Dactyl[8]! She gets the cashews from Snickers Dactyl's[9] foods bowls and drops them in my foods bowls! Eurekaed! Snack Attack Dactyl Delivery can't be beat.

Dactyls are tricky to train. Not as tricky as moms, but tricky. Tricky like squeezing into a water bowl to take the water bowl baths.

January 14th, 2014

Did you know you can't unexplode an exploded phonesbook? I tried. Twice. It didn't work at the alls.

Exploded phonesbook is all over the floor now. I can't have all that exploded in my tree tent. It fits mom's floor better. It's the good thing mom likes brooming, and picking things up all the time.
Whoa! Dogheads just ran around the corner and into the exploded phonesbook piles. FeLOLING!!!

---

[8] Butters is a female Blue and Gold Macaw. She's turning 9 this year. Sweet, lazy, lovable and totally trainable as all B&G tend to be. She and Felix have a good friendship.

[9] Snickers is a male Scarlet Macaw. Untrainable, stubborn, devoted to his human dad and inside the Felix view, useless. He's turning 7 this year. His nickname is TwoHandsFull.

It's the good thing mom likes brooming, picking things up, and moving the furnitures back all the time.

UH-OH! Dogheads just ran back the other ways through what they didn't run into the first times! FeLOLing!! Doghead crashed into the dactyl tree stand and spilled all the water out! It's the good thing mom likes, brooming, mopping, picking things up, and moving the furniture back all the time.

I'm going into the Felix tent. I'm pretty the sure mom will be on her last nerve endings when she sees a doghead with a garbage can on his head in the middle of wet exploded phonesbooks. I could be wrong. But I doubt it.

January 22nd, 2014

I found the amazing thing in my Felix Box o'Excitements today. Mom called it the Burrito Paper Roll[10]. I call it the Talons of Fury Ripp'n Roar'n Tuber!

It fits my feets and inside is all the good stuffs. I can't believe mom thought of this by herself.

It is the days like this that give me the faiths that one day, I will train all the confused out of her.

What a day for The Felix! I have to get back to my Ripp'n Roar'n Tuber.

February 14th, 2014

---

[10] A foot toy built as follows; Tear a newspaper into long 6" wide strips. Roll the length of the papers adding nuts, wood beads, and other favorites. Once rolled stuff into a half-length of paper towel cardboard roll. Modify the inserted treats and items to your parrot's taste. For Felix a Burrito Paper Roll lasts a few days. Which is saying something for a foot toy meeting a parrot!

Valentine's Day inspires The Felix's muse as much as Santa Claus.

Snickers is Red.
Butters is Blue.
There are two dactyly dactyls in this house, how ridiculous.

Happy Felixtimes Day!

I am thinking of you,
And all the training you have left to do!

Grey Strength to my friends and their work left undone.
Mom and Dad do not need to know, we all think it is fun.

Kiss our beaks, rub our feets, forget the training we're exhausted anyway.

February 17th, 2014

It was about this time Felix and I began traveling to teach. We brought his new travel cage home to mixed reviews. Calling it the Felix RV helped. Context is everything. Almost.

Well she brought home The Felix Recreationaling Vehicle.

I'm not getting in that unless there's pistachios, dipp'n sauce, pretzel stickels, and a Felix Mini RV Box o'Excitements.

March 9th, 2014

Shenanigans outside Felix's windows are always of concern. Spring of '14 presented three months of frustration after I put out a bird feeder. Squirrels and all manner of bird showed up testing every nerve Felix owned.

Bird Feeder. That's what mom says is that thingy hanging off my tree outside in my yard. I am a bird. Where's my bird feeder?

Her bird feeder is broken. It is a squirrel feeder. Maybe she bought the wrong feeder, I don't know. But the birds are fighting the squirrels and the squirrels are hanging on the feeder like Godzilla hangs on buildings fight to planes.

Nothing good can come from this.

I can't see what is in there, but it better not be Felix Pistachios. Godzilla squirrels are fighting, falling, climbing, and fighting again. I wouldn't do that unless there was Felix Pistachios in there.

I need a Felix Feeder Thingy in here. Away from Godzilla squirrels of the course.

March 17th, 2014

Felix had adopted a poor attitude about Mondays. Like most of us.

I have the idea!

If every thebody ignores Monday it will go away! Do not even look at it! Then dad stays, and I get more pistachios and fizzy drinks. And then dad can open the garage and I can help him build the things out there.

It will be Feeday! I better get dad and explain how we can fix this annoying.

Ironicalies FeeDay is alsotoo, Saint Patrick's Day. Here is a Paddy Poem I wrote with The Guy's Pen.

May you never forget what is worth remember'in,
Nor ever remember what's best forgotten.

Like remember'in the fizzy drinks n' forget'n the Mondays!

March 24th, 2014

I watched the Cosmos TV with mom and dad.

AstroFizzysist Neil deGrasse Tyson did not talk about Planet Felix one time. How ridiculous! The NASA names a planet The Felix. I waited and waited and watched and waited. Planet Felix is right out there in the space! AstroFizzysist Tyson did not even point at it one time.

Alsotoo, Milkyways are candy bars. They are not in the space. They are at the grocery stores.

AstroFizzysist must be a fancy word for ridiculous...phtttt. Candy bars in space. AstroFizzysist Neil deGrasse Tyson, you are hilarious!

March 29th, 2014

Spring. Felix seeks the comforts in the odd and not recommended places.

I love slipper. This loving affair is getting awkward. Dad keeps putting his feet in slipper. Last night slipper was my girlfriend all night and then I threw up in her. So romantical. Then dad put slipper on his foot. How awkward for him.

I dated towel for a whiles. She was nice and soft and didn't say much.

Then mom brushed her teeth and wiped her mouth all over towel. I had to break up after that.

I tried dating dad's black socks. They ran off all the times. I want a serious relationshiper. Not the one foot stand.

Finding a girlfriend is hard.

April 10th, 2014

The squirrels put a little squirrel flag on the bird feeder. Obviouslies they invaded. Now it's a squirrel invasion I do not have the time for.

I told mom, bird feeders are not for birds. They are for invasionings. And now there's a little flag with a squirrel on it that is holding his squirrel fist up screaming victories. So. Many. Squirrels.

Twitchy jumpy floofy-tailed squirrel invaders. Next thing will be them crashing the door and heading to the Felix Jar of Pistachio Snacks and sticking their squirrel cootie flag on it.

I could have told mom this would happen. But nobody asks the Felix.

April 21st, 2014

Mom put a "kiddie" pool on the bird room table and put the waters in it with floating rubber ducks. She calls it a dactyl toy of fun. I call it Proof It Is Monday Again. Mondays are hard for her.

She says the dactyls will love splashing in their fun pool.

First I say she is mopping up after dactyls, mumbling soon, and alsotoo, what is a kiddie? And is it in my room now? These are the things I know and want to know.

April 23rd, 2014

Spring is just a struggle for parrots as it is for the humans in the room.

Butters Dactyl borfered on mom today. She just up and regurgitatered on mom's shoulder. Mom says it is because Butters is saying "I love you!" to her.

Snickers Dactyls pooped on her shirt. I wonder what Snickers is saying with that other end of a dactyl?

Felix Favorites Food Recipe - approved April 25th, 2014

Felix's Faux French Fry Fun!

You'll need:

- 1 plastic baggie
- 1 Idaho Potato
- 1 tablespoon Olive Oil

Your favorite parrot seasonings and herbs. Finely chop any fresh herbs you wish to use.

PreHeat oven to 300 degrees (148C)

Cut potato lengthwise to create potato wedges or french fry shapes with skin on.

Put seasonings, Olive Oil and potato in a Ziploc baggie and shake it up!

Spread out potato pieces on a cookie sheet and place in the oven.

Cooking time varies depending on the cut of the potato and how crispy you want to make them. Flip with spatula every few minutes to get all sides even.

Let cool. Serve. Enjoy the quiet.

Felix's favorite seasonings are ground pepper corn, parsley, dill, and basil.

I use Flax Oil, you may prefer coconut or EVO, or the like to crisp the potatoes.

Felix's Favorites Food Recipe 2 - approved May 6th, 2014

Felix's ApplePopcorn Treats

Quantities vary according to preferred serving size. You cannot save this recipe successfully, so create just enough.

- popcorn
- apple
- watercress
- broccoli
- baby carrots

Finely chop apples, watercress, broccoli and baby carrots. Mix and fold into a paper towel. Gently roll the chop around the paper towel to remove excess moisture.

Add popcorn and chop into a bowl together, toss. Serve.

This was Felix's favorite today. Tomorrow it will change. But making just popcorn and apples is never wrong. Anytime.

May 14th, 2014

Mom is thinking alone again. She forgot that all the best and biggest bird toys in the worlds are not as good as attentions. One toy is more fun when we can play and train together, then a zamillion toys alone. Because playing is training.

The Felix is hilarious! She needs training. I made the schedulings to make sure she laughed and and trained today.

How can she forget any of this?

Felix Favorites Food Recipe - approved May 16th, 2014

Lettuce Entertain You!

You'll need:

- Big leafy butter lettuce leaves
- Pine Nuts/Walnut pieces/pistachio pieces (whatever floats your boat, but chopped)
- Chopped sweet peppers in yellow, red, and orange.
- Fresh carrot strings (you know, run your carrot peeler over a carrot and there ya go!)
- Black Bean Hummus
- Cottage Cheese

Add Black Bean Hummus to carrot strings, nut pieces, and sweet peppers to get a clumpy sticky hummus evenly mixed.

Spoon into a leaf of Butter Lettuce.

Lay the full lettuce leaf in a regular pellet bowl so that the clump of mix sits centered in the leaf and bowl. (pretty!)

Top with a bit of Cottage Cheese.

Felix Favorites Foods Recipe - approved July 9th, 2014

Almond Milk Ice Creamy Dream.

3 Cups Unsweetened Almond Milk (the kind with nothing but almond milks, none of that guar gum and additives stuff)

- 1/2 cup mashed blueberries
- 1/2 diced strawberries
- 1/4 applesauce* (the kind with just apples)

You can make your own applesauce by skinning, chopping an apple and mashing it with a potato masher or put your food processor to work.

Pour almond milk and fruits and apple sauce into a freezable container, stir. Put in the Freezer. Wait 1 hour, take it out, stir it up a bit, put it back in the freezer. Freeze overnight.

You can use nuts and pumpkin seeds and other fruits, too. Now you have an Ice Creamy treat for your feet that is okay to eat!

Felix Favorites Foods Recipe - approved July 22nd, 2014

- Orangey Icy Treat Bowls!
- One orange
- Veggie Juice OR Fruit Juice
- Whatever chopped nuts your Trainer likes.

Cut the top 1/8 off an orange, now scoop out the innards without hurting the skin.

Chop up and mash the orange innards and mix with your favorite juice. Add chopped nuts or whatever else. Pour all that back into the orange skin bowl.

FREEZE it in the Freezer inside a baggie.

Once it's frozen you can cut it into wedges (BE CAREFUL!) Or you can just hand it over to a big bird. Dactyls like the whole thing at once.

Felix Favorites Food Recipe - approved September 25th, 2014

YAPPLE POPCORN!!

Oh it's for real. It's delicious!!

You need:

- Popcorn
- Cashews
- 1/2 an apple (no skin)
- 1 cup apple sauce

Pop popcorn.

Crunch up cashews to small bits (or bites depending on the size of your Trainer).

Chop up the apple and stir into apple sauce. NOW it's Yappley!

Stir the cashews up into the yapple sauce.

Now stir THAT into the popcorn. Yapple Popcorns!

Depending on your Trainer's preferences you can go gooey to slightly wet.

Please consult your Personal Trainer for preferred details.

October 12th, 2014

I wrote mom a poem today. To help her on her way. (out of confused)

Roses are red.
Violets are blue.
My face is empty.
What's wrong with this picture?

June 16th, 2016

Felix was busy emergency training me out of my deep confused (I almost died of confused) in 2015. After stabilizing my confused to acceptable livable trainable levels, he found himself nominated by the Parrot Party to run the ticket for Presidential. This decision proved pivotal to his belief in The Confused and just how much it mucks up all the works.

It is my duty to accept The Parrot Party Nominationings for Parrot Party Presidential Candidate for 2016!

Also, for the records, this presidenting cannot interrupt my breakfasts. I can't president with the low blood sugars.

Vote FELIX! *** Vote CHANGE! *** Vote Pistachios!

Thank you for my Supports!

If I am elected Presidential, my first orderings of the businesses will be to declare politicians fired and alsotoo, unemployed. They can apply for the unemployment benefits if they want. Because I am not asking the peoples to pay for politicians. That is ridiculous!

After that, everything else should work.

I am the Candidate to get rid of The Confused!

June 30th, 2016

June 30th, Felix chose Kirby Lurker as his running mate for the Vice Presidential. Running on the platform of confused and criminaling activities, Kirby was a natural choice. Kirby took a moment out of his busy lurking schedule to campaign for Felix in the birdroom.

As your Vice Presidentialing Lurker I will take on the issue of Illegal Blanket Worms[11]!

October 13th, 2016

As the election grew closer, Felix's campaign speeches caught on fire! The cheers and hubbubing were alive in all 50 States.

Things you can count on not happening if I am elected Presidential.

1) Confused
2) Ridiculous
3) Annoying
4) More Confused
5) Cat grabbing
6) Emailing
7) More Ridiculous
8) Walls to stop Tunnels
9) Talk that doesn't do anything
10) More Annoying
11) Confused debating Ridiculous
12) Early bedtime

---

[11] Some refer to these as strings on blankets. But we all know they are worms needing to be arrested or eliminated.

13) Broccoli touching Orange chunks
14) Mixed colors in pellet bags
15) Leftover Confused
16) Politicians (I think we know why)

Things you can count on happening if I am elected the Presidential.

1) Anti-Confused Task Force
2) Anti-Ridiculous Task Force
3) Anti-Annoying Task Force
4) Everybody gets goats through the Goats4Votes Universal Goat Program!
5) Everything just working pretty good after The Confused, ridiculous, and annoying politicians are gone.

November 1st, 2016

The campaign bug bit The Felix. He found his voice and purpose for after breakfast and before lunch. His final campaign speech will live on in the history of historical Presidentialing Campaigns.

Greetings Registering Voters and Delegates, Grey Strength to you!

As we are looking down the roads to the end of the end of all this confused I am here this mornings to reassure you! I am sure I am the best to vote for, that's for sure. The Felix Administration is TOUGH on confused.

I am sure those other guys are ridiculous. After all this blahblahblahing, there is no arguing they are really good at being annoying. They are like the Typhoid Mary! Only you catch the confused!

I am sure the goats are on the boards for the Double Goat Anti Confused Project. Take Two Goats and laugh! Confused hates laughing. Remember your goats will be looking for their cake.

I am sure once we get rid of The Confused, everything will work pretty good! I am, alsotoo, sure that somewhere between cat grabbing and emailing the servers Registering Voters forgot what was really importants. Being nice. It is easy to get distracted when confused and ridiculous are on the speakers. I know. I watch mom dance to her speakers and there is nothing but confused going on there!

So Vote Felix! Let's be nice together! Do not listen to ridiculous things that only make confused things. I am sure a Vote for Felix is a Vote for NOT confused ever again. And I am really sure that no matter the what, if we stay together and not give into the confused, everything can be all the right.

Vote FELIX! Vote CHANGE! Bring Pistachios!

Speaking of pistachios, did you know that pistachios are the one of the oldest nuts and that pistachios help with the low blood sugars and the diabetes? You didn't? Now you do!

A Vote for Felix is a vote for information you can use!

A Vote for Felix is MORE Pistachio trees planted!

Thank you for my supports! Thank you for your votes!

Let's get confused out of the Washingmachine DC, and let's put a Grey in the White House!

I am Felix R LaFollett and I am running for the Offerings of the Presidential of the United States!

January 3rd, 2017

After conceding the Presidentialing Campaign to the other guy, Felix moved forward with other matters. All of which existed upstairs, in the master bathroom, on the counter. And in the sink.

I set the sails on the Felix yellow submariner this mornings. After I arrested toothbrush, toothbrush holder, and cup for trespassing on the Felix submarine. They bounce on the floor louder than I thought. Mom showed up and said, "What are you doing in the sink Felix?"

"It's Felix submarine. It does not sink."

"Felix! Why are all my things on the floor? Now I need a new toothbrush."

"Well, tell your thingys to stop breaking the laws."

"Why is the towel in the sink with you? Did you do that on purpose?"

"Firstlies, the towel is in the Felix submariner because it is comfortables. Secondlies, my submariner does not sink. Alsotoo, of the course on purpose. I have the good ideas. And alsotoo, too, there is a hole in my submariner. Did you open that hole?"

"Look, if you're staying in there Felix, let me close the stopper so it doesn't poke your feet."

"The Felix Talons of Fury thank you."

I hope she remembers all this later, so she doesn't forget she already knows.

January 30th, 2017

Due to manufacturing snafus or The Confused, yellow pellet ratios spiked in early 2017 setting off a cascade of concern, counting, and tossing.

You don't get elected the Presidential and The Confused explodes! Yellow Pellet Ratios are emergency levels! No thebody knows why. Oh look, how did that happen?

CONFUSED that's how.

I counted the yellow pellets in my foods bowls, yellow pellet ratio is unacceptables. I had no choices but to throw them all out and into doghead faces and the floor. Dogheads snortled up the yellow pellets like that fish at the bottom of the aquariums that has the face that sticks to the glass.

This tells you every the thing you need to know about dogheads.

Felix began working on his book, Directions for the Confused, *as well as this memoir of* A Felix in the Time of Confused. *He decided to work local on The Confused. Mainly, me. Mom is the test case proving the eradication of confused is, difficult.*

He invested himself in all things local and annoying from the beginning of 2017 until September 2018 where he stepped forward and into the fast approaching, completely confused, Covid covered, off it's rocker, Presidentialing Campaign for 2020.

September 9th, 2018

I perch before you this evenings to announce my candidacy for the Presidentialing of the United States. Because The Confused can't win!

I also announce my choice of the running mate for Vice Presidentialing of Angus Lee LaFollett. First, dogs run fast. So running he can do for the Parrot Party!

Two, Vice Presidentials really only just sit, stay, and roll over any theway. So this works out for both of us.

In the coming days I will be announcing all kinds of not confused Presidentialing kind of announcements. But know this, Candidate Felix R. LaFollett will not bring confused into the White House. Because I'm going to call it the Grey House so nobody gets confused.

I will also be announcing my goals for my Presidentialing Plans. Confused is running the rampant! I pledge to get the confused OUT of the Grey House!

First! Every thebody who wants a goat, gets a goat. Because nobody doesn't like a goat for a friend.

Thank you for my supports!

I am, Presidentialing Candidate, Felix R. LaFollett

It immediately became evident that Felix needed to focus on Christmas, his requirements, and making sure Santa knew these things.

Correspondence 12/14/18 through 12/28/18 between Felix R. LaFollett and Mr. Santa Claus

Merry the Christmas and Grey Strength to you Santa The Claus!

I am sending you this Felix Letter of Explanations and Requirements so that you can take care of the business of clausing.

Things Felix needs:

And first I think it is important to bring up the fact that mom is wrong. I do not want things, I need them to be The Felix. Like a fish needs the fish bowl full of waters to fish. How can I possibly Felix without these Felixy things I need to Felix. I am sure you are understanding of this, but mom can confuse just about anybody. This concerns me.

Any theway...

Things Felix needs to Felix:

1) A new spatula. And not a metal spatula that irritates my ears when dad is spatulating pancakes. I need the rubbery soft kind that flips and folds scrambling eggs and pancakes without giving me the headaches of annoying.

2) A new tent towel. Not red. Not green. Not yellow of course. That would be ridiculous.

3) A membership to Pistachios for Felix Club. It's a monthly club that sends the Felix (that's me) pistachios so the Felix Jar does not go low. I hate it when that happens. Mom's sense of urgency and priorities always lets the Felix Jar of Treats for the Feets go so low, I'm pretty sure I'm going to die of the low blood sugar. You don't even know Santa, how many times I have escaped death at the nick of time. (No punning intended)

4) Another SaturDADday. I don't care where you put it but I think it's time for another one of those.

5) A goat. Maybe two goats. Mostly because watching mom chase the doghead is getting old. This will be good entertainments.

6) I read somewhere that you are magical, and you have elves and flying reindeer, so I think you can handle this next one. I need yellow pellets abolished, unless another trainer likes them, but I don't. I think maybe a laser beam in my tent that only shoots yellow pellets would be helpful. Or maybe just write a Santa Letter to the confused people making pellets that FELIX does not want yellow pellets in his breakfast. I will let you decide between the letter of recommendationings and the laser beam.

7) A new warm tea cup. Somehow things got weirdo around here and mom serves warm tea to Felix in a yellow tea cup. (see item 6)

8) A water pistol. Specifically a water cannon pistol to attach to my Felix Tent so I can shoot Snickers Dactyl. This will be hilarious, and also entertainments. (see item 5 for the importants of entertainments)

9) A new phonesbook. Just in the case I blow up the phonesbooks I already have. And alsotoo, can I have a North Pole Phonesbook?

10) A new FeeTV Snack Attack Table. The one I have is too small. I can barely fit the snack attacks I need on there and not trip over them. How can I FeeTV Movie View safe if I'm tripping over treats in the dark? I cannot. I could fall off my FeeTV Snack Attack Table AND die of the low blood sugars at the same time! (see item 3 for other threats)

This will get you started Santa the Claus. If I think of any other Felix needs to Felix I will write another letter to you.

You're welcome.

Felix R. LaFollett
Trainer, Author, Presidentialing Candidate, Hawk King

During the holiday season, Felix grew suspicious of the neighbor's coming and goings. He also felt Santa might be in danger. To whit, Felix's presents were in danger.

December 18th, 2018

Dear Santa Claus,

It's me, Felix.

I have to warn you about Weirdo Neighborling and his blinky Christmas lights. And his lighted up balloon reindeer under the tree by the front door. And those giant candy canes, that are not real candy canes, hanging all over the places. And that thing that might be an elf, but could also be a Swedish mountain climber that fell down the mountain or maybe another reindeer that lost two legs and all the antlers.

IT'S ALL A TRAP!

Do not fall for it Santa Claus. Because yesterday I saw weirdoling pretending to mow his grasses and you know what I think he was REALLY doing out there? I think he was putting down a Santa snatching net that will snatch you when you try to walk on it to look at those balloon reindeer! And then do you know what I think will happen? I think you will be hanging upside down in a net from a tree looking at fake giant candy canes upside down!

Alsotoo, I have seen some things you do not want to know about going on over there. Like one day their doghead was digging holes all the day. And then weirdoling came with a shovel and started filling them up! But do you know what I think was really going on over there in those doghead holes? I think they were burying the Easter Bunny. I do. Because nobody has seen him since. That's cereal evidential right there!

I am concerned about your well faring Santa Claus. How do you know that your lists are right? Maybe a naughty someone stole the identities of a nice someone and then you know what I think? I think you will go down the chimney of a naughty someone's house and end up in the basement surrounded by weirdo. Because your list was wrong! Do you trust elves to make your list? I've seen pictures of them. They are small. Their brains can't be big. Are you sure you can trust a list made by elves with tiny brains? If I had elves do you know what I would do? I would make them take a smart test. To see just how much smart is in that tiny brain. Then I would know if their listings are smart, or just a little smart.

So I would just not trust your elves. It's the smartest thing to do until you get the testings done. And do not go to Weirdo Neighborlings house. If you have to, take some elves. They are expendables.

Oh! Alsotoo, and one more thingy:

Please add a new Felix Ultra Box o'Excitements to my listings of needs not wants. I have used the Felix Box o'Excitements all year, I really need the Ultra one for the next year because I am running for the Presidentialing of the United States and you can't Presidential with a regular toy box.

I hope you take me cereal about the Weirdo Neighborling and the elves. I am concerned.

Grey Strength! Merry the Christmas!

Felix R LaFollett
Author, Trainer, 2020 Presidentialing Candidate, Concerned Nice Listing

P. theS.

I can't leave cookies out for you, or the milk. Mom says they are bad for you. But I can leave dipp'n sauce and pretzel stickels and I will. They will be right by my tent on the FeeTV Snack Attack Table that you are going to replace with the new bigger one I asked for in the last Dear Santa Letter. Dipp'n sauce is delicious!

December 24th, 2018

Dear Santa the Claus,

You probably know what day today is, but in the case you don't it is the day before the Christmas Delivery Day. I forgot some thingys I need to Felix. It's the good thing you can handle the pressure.

Thingys I forgot. I need to Felix.

11) Pistachios. I didn't say anything the last times because you should know this...but then I thought, "Wowzy! Mom should know many things and she doesn't. Maybe Santa has the confused like mom!" I am here to help!

12) Bottle caps. These are hilarious. I can squeeze them and they pop out of my beak and make the "POP!" sound. I need these.

13) More dad. One more SaturDADday PLUS a bonus DADday. Maybe you add more times in a day, maybe you add more days in the weeks or maybe we change Wednesday to PLUS Bonus DADday. Wednesday is boring.

14) The Steiner 20x80 Military Binoculars with the superior low light performance and waterproof case, to keep the Military Specs on Weirdo Neighborling.

Speaking of the Weirdolings next door...

They added a giant blow up snow globey with dancing penguins stuck inside next to the giant hanging candy canes that are not real at all. I do not think the penguins are dancing. I think they are TRAPPED! I think they are trapped and looking for the escape hatch from the giant snow globey. Be CAREFUL! Do not end up like a penguin trapped in a giant snow globey.

I am so cereal about this right thenow. Who traps penguins in giant snow globeys? Serial Santa Killers. That's who.

I will try to fire smoke canisters and orange flares of danger in Weirdo Neighborling's front yard after they go to the sleep. Maybe you could get my Steiner 20x80 Military Binoculars here early so I can fire ordinances with more accuracies and certainties. I do not want to blow up the trapped penguins.

One more thingy,

15) I need a cloaking device to disappear when dactyls are annoying. There's no point in waiting for them to stop being dactyls. Maybe not a cloaking device. Maybe a disappearing cabinet like I saw on the FeeTVMovie last night. That would be handy.

That's about it.

Be careful tonight flying around with that sleigh and those eight tiny reindeer. That all sounds sketchy any theway.

Grey Strength! Merry theChristmas!

You're welcome, again.

Felix R LaFollett
Author, Hawk King, 2020 Presidentialing Candidate, Christmas Presents Recipient on the Nice List

After Christmas, Felix took inventory of his gifts from Santa. He waited a few days before writing and tread lightly on the subject of missed opportunities and gifts.

December 27th, 2018

Dear Santa the Claus,

I am writing to let you know you forgot my goats. Thank you for my spatula, and Ultra Box o'Excitements full of Stuffs. But you forgot the goats. This is not about the Felix. I am worried about mom. This is about mom. So you know I am being very thoughtful and nice right now. Right after the Christmas where you forgot my goats.

You see, mom needs goats. She says so all the time, Well not all the time, just when doghead steals a pillow and won't give it back. She yells, "Angus! I will put you on a train heading to a boat that's heading to Cuba and get goats instead! They are easier than you, sir."

Sir. Who calls a doghead sir? FeLOL.

Any theway. She needs these goats for the entertainments. It just so happens that if she is entertaining, I am entertaining, too. So if you could get the goats you are really getting Christmas presents for two nice listings at the same time. Which is pretty economicaled and easier on your eight tiny reindeer. I am assuming mom is also on the nice list. She's confused, but not naughty confused. That would be the Weirdo Neighborlings next door.

Oh! Which reminds me. You aren't in their basement right now are you? They took all their Santa Claus traps down, but I suppose that could mean they caught you in a smelly basement, or maybe a closet with a mop and bucket and two cans of bug sprays. I dunno. I'm just guessing. They look like weirdos with bugs. If you are reading this in their basement or the mop closet with the bug spray, try to find Easter Bunny in there. Rabbits can dig better than a doghead. I know. I have a rabbit for a friend. I think you could fit in a rabbit tunnel.

If you are reading this sitting on your santa chair at the North Pole, never themind.

Alsotoo, I should say we need these goats now. Not the next year. Just in case you are thinking I can wait. Maybe I can, but I do not want to take any chances on mom not being entertaining. This is about mom. Not the Felix. I really care about mom's goats. For mom. Not the Felix.

You're welcome,

Felix R LaFollett
Author, 2020 Presidentialing Candidate, Personal Trainer to the Confused, Nice List Member for 2019, Hawk King

Santa responded the first day of his 363 days of vacation. Proving he is both efficient and timely in correspondence.

December 28, 2018

Dear Felix,

Thank you for all your letters. They were very helpful to my work, and for the elves. You are a very helpful Felix.

As far as the goats. We've had this discussion before. If you remember during your 2016 Presidential Campaign you inquired about the logistical delivery services of Claus Industries. As we stated then, delivering goats is tricky business. You had promised two goats for each of your constituents and those that voted for you. That's quite a load of goats. But the facts do not change, no matter the number of goats.

As we discussed in our letter of October 17, 2016 transporting goats requires picking up goats first. There are no goats at the North Pole. What with the elves and the reindeer there just isn't enough space. That and Mrs. Claus is allergic to goats. Which isn't a strong excuse considering she's allergic to the elves. Allergies notwithstanding, goat delivery is tricky.

I'll remind you of your letter of October 26, 2016, although convincing on the surface, overlooked the important logistical matter of acquisition and comfort of the goats while in sleigh transport. I did appreciate the idea of hot air balloons attached to their Christmas bows. That was creative! And with more investigation possibly viable. But there is the important matter of comfort for the goats. I had Dasher in the sleigh once. Sitting in a sleigh proved problematic. He threw his back out over Siberia.

I feel confident in saying a goat and a reindeer fold up in about the same way. I doubt sleigh transport is the proper choice.

I would suggest an idea close to home, and that will keep you in charge of all the goat goings-on. I am sure there are adoptable goats in rescues near you. I know of one donkey and goat at the SPCA in your area. I know a donkey is not part of your plans, but you might want to be open minded about these things. I hear donkeys can be quite entertaining.

Finally, I also received your text about transporting goats for your 2020 Presidential Campaign Promises and Ideas. (That's quite a title for a Felix running for President). We have 2 years to consider viable transport mechanisms as well as gathering homeless goats from rescue. This may be possible. If we get a jump on planning. I may be able to work in your two personal goats, if you can wait until 2020. I understand the pressure you are under entertaining your mom.

Claus Industries does ask for a 10% down payment to ensure contractual agreements. From my calculations that will be a Promissory Note of Being Good and Nice for 5 years in a row. I can send the paperwork to you via FedEx. Which I do not recommend for goats. Paperwork, yes. Goats, no.

I hope you enjoy your spatula and Dad Pancakes all this year.

Please let me know if you would like a cost investigation and process accumulation data sheet on the 2020 Goats 4 Votes initiative.

I'll get the paperwork together for the contractual agreements and down payment.

Ho HO HO!

Santa Claus
CEO Claus Industries

January 17th, 2018

Square is square and round is round and that other shape is wrong. That other shape that is not square is always wrong and I told mom it was wrong the first day I threw all the cantaloupies on the floor.

What part of Door Knocking-Dog Whistle-Back Up The Truck-Seagull Yelling doesn't she understand?

Here I am, supervisoring her chopping and cutting and what do I get? The other shape not square. I suppose a round cantaloupie would make the untrained trainee think that all the parts inside are round, if they think alone. Which she is doing with me in the room. I told her a long time ago do not think alone, I am here! Just don't do it.
What part of Head Spin Shake, Water Bowl Dump, Food Toss, Wing Flap, Old Grumpy Guy Growl doesn't she understand? I made myself very the clear.

Here I sit full of round cantaloupies. I had no choice. It was the low blood sugars dying or eating round cantaloupies. I will probably end up with the indigestionings and refluxors.

Alsotoo, speaking of the indigestionings. Did you see what the Kirby did to The Felix yesterday? I was ready to deliver my Epic Speech of The Felix. He was supposed to stay upstairs and throw everything in the sink. But noooo, Kirby shows up and takes over my video time and speech. Mom just shrugged and smiled. You can't be more confused than that.

This is exactlies why I fired the Kirby and asked Angus Doghead to be my Vice Presidential Runnermate. Because all you have to do is sit, stay, and roll over when you are Vice Presidenting. Just sit, pant alot if you have to, but sit.

I have to get mom in line. She's delirious and unstabled. First thing after lunch I am throwing everything out of my Box o' Excitments. Then I will throw the Box o'Excitements on the floor. Explode my phonesbook, on the floor. Throw all the dactyl foods on my Felix Weirdo Neighborling Observatory, on the floor. Take a water bowl bath, and throw all the water on the floor. Fly nine times to the stairs when she thinks she is thinking. I can have a word with her during Taxi Service back to my cage.

Which I will then make sure to say, Crow Calling-Dog Barking-Ambulance-Back Up The Truck-Laserbeam-Bomb Drop Explosion-Door Knocking-Head Spinner.

If she can't understand that, I will have to train all the way back to the beginning. How annoying.

In the Spring of 2018 Felix fell ill with a clogged nose and sinus infection. This required multiple doctor visits, nasal flushes, and medication. They say a man's strength is measured against his grit. Felix's grit is grey, but very much on his last nerve ending.

March 13th, 2018

Doctor stole my boogers. With a Felix Booger Picker! And then she put them in tubes to share with other doctors somewhere else. She says they have to grow more boogers to see what my boogers are made of so I can get the right medicine. I told her it's the right medicine if it's inside the vanilla ice creamers. She didn't listen. She wants to grow booger trees. Felix Booger Trees.

Alsotoo, I was tortured. Nose hosing is not something in the trainee bathroom. It's the Felix. In a smelly clown towel, upside down, with water squirted up my nose hole, and my other nose hole dripping into a bowl to catch Felix Boogers.

Why? Obviously she wants to make a forest of Felix Booger Trees. What a weirdo!

I had the vanilla ice creamers and medicines last night. Which wasn't good enough for all this nose hosing booger business. Mom said something about nose drops to pick up at the drug store. I refuse to drop my nose anywhere.

I have decided doctor cannot keep my Felix Booger Trees. Those are mine and I want them back.

When I wake up from my next Felix nap I'm going to throw all my foods bowls on the floor. I am going to murder my bell. And I will make sure mom sees I am not looking at her unless she has my vanilla ice creamers medicine spoon. That's the only time I am looking at her. And if she has the popcorns. Or maybe pasta wheelies. Definitely not when she has nothing.

I better get my Felix Booger Trees back.

March 19th, 2018

Friday the nights I escaped from the burrito smelly towel dad tried to trap me in and flew to the stairs to hide. Doghead narked on me and dad trapped me again. Nose hole drips are ridiculous! Doghead is a rat.

This Felix Booger Business is out of the hand. SaturDADday I was forced to take extreme actionings. I have decided the right ice creamers is the wrong ice creamers. HA! That will teach her and her nose drop dripping. I am not a burrito to be smelly towel burritoed to have the drips dropped into my nose hole!

I caught her attempting to trick the Felix on the Sunday. She was putting the medicines in my senior nutriberriballs.

So I threw them on the floor. Doghead ate them. I hope he gets Felix Boogers the size of a Weirdo.

I caught her other trick on Sunday night. She put the medicine on my pistachios. WHAT!? I gave her the Eye of Irritated and kicked them off my Snack Attack Table while giving her the Eye of Vengeance.

Unthefortunetly she put the medicine on my senior nutriberriballs alsotoo, and I ate those while I kicked poisoned pistachios on the floor. I have to keep the Eye of Suspicions on her from now on, she can't be trusted at all.

My nose hole keeps opening and closing with the Felix Boogers. She keeps looking at my face. Her head is huge!

Wednesday I have to take the Felix RV[12] in the clown car[13] back to the doctor and get my Felix Booger Trees back. If I don't get those back I will start a mutiny with all the other parrots in there. I'm starting with that dactyl I heard. He sounded annoyed anyway.

March 31, 2018

As I suspected the ride in the Felix RV in the clown car ended up RIGHT back where I started. Things took a turn for the weirdo right away.

First mom and Doctor Noseitall talked about my Grammy. Doctor Noseitall said Felix Booger Trees grew up to be grammy negative, but my grammy was positive but there were no grammy positive booger trees.

---

[12] Felix's travel cage and outdoor napping cage.
[13] 2007 Toyota Tundra. Not a swipe at Toyota products, considering their products were not engineered with the comfort of The Felix in mind.

I have NO idea if I won a Grammy. I should. I have the great Fee Voice.

Any theway, so then I have to stand on a perch and wait for them to realize I am perfectly 452 grams just like the last time. I could have told them that. No one asked. And I still do not know if I won a Grammy. And now I don't know if I have 452 grammies somewhere waiting for me to find them.

Then, Doctor Noseitall says, "Oh Felix let's see what we can find." And boom, shabam, wizz I'm burrito trapped in her smelly Doctor Noseitall towel and she is looking straight at my face. Her head is Ginormousing! I think her head is bigger than mom's. She steals more Felix Boogers and says, "Oh, these don't smell bad!"

Who smells boogers? And then Doctor Noseitall Helper says, "No they don't!" Dynamic Weirdo Duo! For the records, Doctor Noseitall Helper has a big head, alsotoo.

Mom says, "Oh! That's good then."

"Oh yes", says Doctor Noseitall. "Felix probably doesn't have that infection, but we're still going to send these back to the lab and try to grow those Felix Booger Trees. Because sometimes things just don't grow in a lab like they do in a nose. But now he's taking medicine so the Felix Booger Trees will be different than before any theway, but it's good to know we really don't have Grammy Positive Felix Booger Trees."

AND I STILL DO NOT KNOW IF I WON A GRAMMY!

So mom, Doctor Noseitall, and Dr. Noseitall Helper start jabber jibbering about me. As the if anything they are saying out loud makes any sense any theway.

Blah blah blah. I don't know if I have Felix Booger Trees in my nose already... I don't know if I won the Grammy... and I don't know if I have 452 grammies somewhere waiting for me to find them.

Then Dr. Noseitall Helper holds me upside thedown and Doctor Noseitall starts nose hosing again. I am not a faucet!

So I am left with nothing to do but let them know my disatisfactionings with my Grammy winning Fee Voice. THEN Dr. Noseitall says, "Oh Felix, so much drama!"

Right to my face! I should win the Oscar with that Grammy, though.

Doctor Noseitall releases me from her clutches and I walk on the floor over to mom to show her just what she has done to The Felix! And mom says, "Oh Felix. You look like you've been on a bender." And they all laugh at the Felix!

Sufficing to say, I will have my vengeance! After lunch.

March 25th, 2018

After I finallies get mom straightened the out with the ice creamers, treats for drops and treats for drips and the extra warm teas of desperation and groveling, after all that trainings and working Butters Dactyl messes it all up! She is jealous of me. It is obvious.

I could not believe all her poor acting and not very dramaticals. "Oh, Oh it is me! Butters Dactyl and I have something in my eye! Oh the woe is to me! Don't look at FELIX! Look at me and my woe eye!"

And mom did.

Oh sure! Now Felix Boogers are not that importants now. Oh SURE! Butters Dactyl has to go to Dr. Noseitall right away because she has a thingy in her eye or whatever because I don't care and I had mom almost trained and I missed my warm teas of desperation and groveling because Butters Dactyl had go to Dr. Noseitall for whatever I don't care about! Jealous dactyls are ridiculous! I have to start trainings all over! Mom is so distracted she reminds me of a doghead.

What about the Felix? What about my needs? What about the trainings!? What about my Nose Boogers that don't grow trees and I don't have back yet.

And what about the Grammy? Did I win it or the NOT!?!?

Dr. Noseitall says Butter Dactyl has blepharospasm OS and she gets the ice creamers medicine and the eye drips! Oh the sure! Felix only has the nose boogers but Butters Dactyl has the blepharspazoidal blah dee blah! Oh sure my boogers aren't importants now. OH SURE!! Mom has the rights ice cream THIS time. You are welcome for that Butters DactylSpaz.

She walks over to Butters Dactyl and gets all gooeygoober, "Oh Butterbean I'm so sorry your eye hurts, I love you Butterbean. muah.muah.muah." GACK! Mom is ridiculous. She could be making extra warm teas of desperation and groveling but the nooooooo...she's over there petting the head of a poser! POSER!

And so here I am second fiddling to a posing dactyl. All the trainings down the drains. Sharing my ice creamers. Waiting in the line. Sharing the warm teas of desperation and groveling. And then today mom says, "Oh Felix I love you too baby. We're going to go back on Wednesday to see Dr. Noseitall one more time. Hang in there baby."

BABY? I am almost twenty the six! Go back!? What trainings can happen out of this now? Big blue blepharospasm ruined my workings. I better get my booger trees back and they better be planted in my Grammy, too. They owe me that much for all this inconveniencing and annoying.

I am almost so irritatedly I can't eat breakfast. Almost. I will force myself to fight the low blood sugars. But I will have to eat super slow and super irritatedlies.

March 29th, 2018

The problem is she doesn't think I understand the words coming out of her mouth. The other problem is Dr. Noseitall does not think I understand the words coming out of her mouth. The other other problem is they think this at the same time in the same place while talking about the Felix in front of The Felix. I heard all their words and they are all confused!

Dr. Noseitall who I am now referring to as Dr. Weirdo Nosepicker, said over and over "I want that piece Felix. You can do this! I want that piece of booger! It's the last one. You look great!"

First, who says this out louds!? Secondlies, where are my Felix Booger Trees? Lasts, yes of the course I look good, I am The Felix. And your head is huge!

Mom says nothing. She sits there watching this debacling but I can read her minds. She's thinking about not Felix!

Then Dr. Noseitall hoses my nose and invites mom over to watch and see my nose drip! And then mom does! And then they are both there watching my nose drip and saying, "ooooh!" and "ahhhhh!" and nodding their huge heads like upside down bobblyheads.

Oh, I know words all theright. Words like traitor, confused, ridiculous, Felix Booger Tree thief!

And THEN, as the if the Felix hasn't already put up with enoughs, Dr. Noseitall releases me from my smelly bondage burrito and she says, "He looks great. I think this is our last time. But I want to give another drug in the case the idea of anaerobic Booger Trees is right. It is only 5% chance but I want to make sure."

I know these words mean nothing is done here at the alls and I better get the right ice creamers the first time!

Alsotoo, IF there are aerobic boogers in my nose doesn't she think I would know this myself!? All that booger jumping. I'm pretty the sure I would notice Felix Boogers jumping around in my face.

And THEN she says, "This medicine tastes really bitter. I was using liver flavor for the cats and they wouldn't eat it. Now I have the fruit loops flavor. But I tried the liver flavor, and decided to go ahead and make everybody unhappy with the fruit loops flavor because no one was happy anyway." WHAT!?!? Are these words even in the right order!? I am not eating livers. I am not Hannibal Lector! I am not eating fruitloopers if it tastes yellow. She knows this.

And what does cats have to do with my nose, my stolen booger trees, or my missing Grammy? Why bring cats into this? I met a cat once, he was rude and snotty. Not snotty like Felix Boogers, but snotty like rude snotty. I wouldn't bring a cat into anything because nothing is going to come from that except a snotty rude cat walking away. That's what they do.

Any theway, so here I am today waiting for livers or fruitloopers or whatever she thinks I don't know about, which I do. I have to start all over on all this trainings. Everything is going on the floor. I will start there.

I may never know where my Felix Booger Trees went. I have no ideas what happened to my Grammy. And now there's Felix aerobic booger trees I didn't even realize were missing until yesterday!
If a cat has those I will have to talk to doghead about hunting. He's supposed to be a hunting dog, but he only ever finds dad's socks. So I don't know if that's the way to go.
But you have to go hunting with the doghead you have, not the doghead you want.

I really want that Grammy. I was going to put it my Felix Box o'Excitements, right under my digesting perch.

Proving focus and effort best fitted for a President, Felix delivered a rousing Campaign Speech just as his personal life had reached a fevered pitch of confused.

March 20th, 2018
Presidentialing Speech to a crowd of alots.

The state of the affairs of The Confused is unacceptables! As the Parrot Party nominee for Presidentialing of the United States I promise to make sure that getting rid of the confused is priorities for my administrations.

(Insert cheers of the agreements with The Felix and yellings of FELIX! FELIX! FELIX!)

Confused is tricky business. First, no one knows they are confused, because they are confused.

To begin the processes of unconfusing our greyt country I will gather the best trainers for my administrations. I urge all my supporters to vote for their local cockatiel congress candidates. Let's get the Congress currently confused, cockatieled! That will fix that.

(Insert Hurrays of the agreements here!)

I also urge all my supporters to vote for their local Senegal senate candidates! Let's get the Senate soppy with serious confused, Senegaled!

(Insert Cheers of the agreements here!)

With the Cockatiel Congress and the Senegal Senate I will also fix the following stuff that everybody says is too hard, which is not, they are just confused.

1) Universal goats! Yes, we can have universal goats. My Goats4Votes! will ensure every supporter that wants a goat, gets 2 goats! Because goats do not like being alone without another goat. Goats help the confused by making them laugh and not worry about things that are not worryables. Because you know the what? The confused is not worryables worried about. Two goats will help everybody!

(Insert cheers and chantings "GOATS! GOATS! GOATS!")

2) Because I do not know this guy Gerry Mandering, that is not a problems at all any theway. VOTE! Gerry won't be around.

(insert Hollers and chants of "Lock Gerry Mandering UP!")

3) From my first day in the Grey House I will make sure all pellets are packaged in one color only. Because I do not like yellow pellets. So there. That's fixed! You can buy oranges, or purples, or blues, or *gack* yellows, or reds and never suffer the High (insert color of hates here) Pellet Ratios AGAIN!

(inserts yells of the reliefs and noddings of agreements!)

As the campaignings continue I will announce more ideas of not confused fixes! I will alsotoo introduce my administrations parrots so you know there is no chance confused is going to show up and start confusing any thebody!

Tomorrow I will be announcing the brand new Felix2020 superPAC (Parrot Action Committee) and asking for your supports! Felix2020 T Shirts with tracking devices will be the availables for you to show your supports of The Felix! (This has nothing to do with World Dominationings. At. All.)

Let's make The United States of the Confused, The United States of the Trainers! Grey Strength! And remembers, I know where you think you are going and I will go first!

(Insert jumping and shouting and hollering and chantings of FELIX! FELIX! FELIX! NO MORE CONFUSED! WE LOVE GOATS!!)

When the history books are written about the political landscape between 2018 and 2020 those historians will have their hands full.

Felix chose to focus specifically on creating the best Felix Administration and Presidential Platform possible. He stepped out of the social media writing for one year and created what most will call "What a parrot would probably do if he could run for president."

Which isn't a bad thing. Considering what the last 45 homosapiens have successfully not accomplished in the history of the United States of Confused.

May 14th, 2019
Presidentialing Speech to a crowd of gazillions.

Grey Strength!

(Insert cheers of hurrahs and hurray here)

As your Presidentialing Parrot Party Candidate I am here to say out loud, there must be Universal Goats!

For far too the long, the House of Representers and the Senating have said there can not be such a thing. Universal Goats is too expensive! Universal Goats can not be done! Universal Goats is a pipe dream! I am here to tell you Goats do not smoke pipes! I don't even know who said that! That's ridiculous.

(Insert cheers of FELIX! FELIX! FELIX!)

It is time to make Universal Goats happen for all. If I am elected President of the United States I will create the American Research Group of Health. ARGH! will help all citizens find the right goats for their needs and the goat's happy. Pre-existing goats or any pre-existing happy will not disqualify each and every citizen from signing up for Universal Goats! Just think ARGH! when you think you are confused or not happy.

(Insert chants of ARGH! ARGH! ARGH! WE NEED GOATS!)

The past administrationings have mislead the truths about Universal Goats and I want to clear that up right the now.

You won't be confused ever with the Felix Administrationings.

(Insert chants of NO MORE CONFUSED!)

Firstly, goats don't care what anybody thinks. They really don't care what anybody thinks about them. So you can say Universal Goats are wrong, but they are not listening to you.

Seconds, "Take two goats and call me in the morning." was first prescribed by Dr. Doolittle in Gary, Indiana on April 11th 1874. Even then doctors were sure Universal Goats could fix a lot.

The patient, confused and a mom, took her two goats and played with them in her backyard all that day. When she woke up the next morning she was happy and had a smile where she once had a frown!

Thirds, Goats turn frowns upside down, obviously.

(Insert chants of UPSIDE DOWN UPSIDE DOWN!)

Five, two goats are better than one goat. The second goat makes sure the first goat ate all the confused by eating the leftover bits while the first goat rests from all of that. Tag Team Universal Goats were first considered the day before Dr. Doolittle told his prescription for the first time. Mostly because the first goat said he didn't want all that responsibility. And his friend Carl said he would help.

(Inserts chantings of CARL! CARL! CARL!)

Six, Goats are forward thinking. Carl proves this.

Nine, Universal Goats is a right. Not a privilege. When someone says to you, OH! Universal Goats can't be for everyone, that's for privilegings only. Remember, that confused everyone is really saying, OH! happy can't be for everyone, happy is only for privilegings. This is ridiculous, I know this because I asked Carl.

Make no mistake or annoying about it. When I am Presidentialing in the Grey House the first thing I will ask my Cockatiel Congress to pay for and the first thing I will ask my Senegal Senate to vote yes for is Universal Goats!

The Goats are ready. The Goats agree. The goats find all this confused annoying, too.

I am Felix R. LaFollett, and I am running for the President of the United States and other places, too. But this is not about World Dominationings. At. All.

Vote Felix! I know where you think you are going, and you are going to need goats to get there!

June 14th, 2019
Presidentialing Campaign Speech to the crowds of cheers and hoots of the hollers.

Grey Strength!

As your Parrot Party Presidentialing Candidate I take my training work super cereal. There is no time for the crepe confusion.

(Insert cheers and chants of NO MORE CONFUSED CREPES!)

Last month I told you about my Goats4Votes initiative. I told you how the goats are ready. I told you how Universal Goats should happen immediatelies for the sake of the confused. I also told you that it's better to have two goats.

(Insert Hurrahs and yells of GOATS ARE GREAT!)

Today, I come before you to discuss the threat of the Low Blood Sugars. This is a issue of National Security. When elected Presidentialing I will create the Department of Blood Sugar Safety and Security. I will appoint the hungriest of trainers to head this department.

(Insert celebrationings of NO MORE LOW BLOOD SUGARS!)

The Low Blood Sugars threaten our world like never before. It is time to recognize that too few snacks and too many ridiculous ideas in foods bowls are threatening our way of the lifes around here! It is time we recognize that high yellow (insert your dreaded colorings here) pellet ratio is a danger, alsotoo!

(Insert yells and cheers and hurrahs! FELIX FELIX FELIX!)

When I am elected the Presidential I will eliminate high dreaded colorings pellet ratios by instituting the "Separate Color Pellet Bags" law with the help of the Senegal Senate. This will alleviation both the confused Trainee shopper AND the high dreaded colorings pellet ratios!

I will also institute and support the Senegal Senate's work to pass the "You Can't Put That in My Foods Bowl, That's Ridiculous" law!

(Insert LOCK UP THE RIDICULOUS! yells and cheers)

Once passed this law will protect your Trainee from making another bowl of confused ever again! We will create the National Ridiculous Foods Bowl Emergency Help Line to support your rights not to have to look at ridiculous thingys in your foods bowls!

Additionalies, by not putting ridiculous things in food bowls we will not be forced to throw things onto the floors! That will save everybody involved time and efforts. Also protecting the nation against the low blood sugars!

Sweeping is exhausting. I'm pretty sure it is. Mom always looks exhausted doing it. Throwing ridiculous ideas on the floors is exhausting! I'm exhausted right now just thinking about it.

(Insert cheers and the adorationings of greyt ideas and NO MORE EXHAUSTION!)

Starting this coming the Monday my campaign will make availables the Felix's Campaign Trail Mix snack attack! Inside you will find the favorite presidentialing tastes AND a free tracking device for your Trainee! Because I know where you think you are going, trainees.

While you snack on cantaloupies, upsidedown broccolis, chopped apples (square, not not square) popcorn and pistachios your Trainee will be immediately synced with the Parrot Party Satelites of where you think you are going! We can beat the low blood sugars! We can beat the confused! We can keep track of trainees better, easier and faster!

(Insert hystericals and crying happy tears of joy and reliefs)

Tomorrow will be better than today if we follow the GREY WAY! Vote Felix!

(Insert jumping up and downs chanting FELIX FELIX FELIX!!)

Thank you for my supports!

I am Felix R. LaFollett and I am running for the Presidentialing of the United States. This has nothing to do with World Dominationings. At. All. Yet.

June 18th, 2019

I don't know where to start so I am going to start at the middle of the beginning where the end hasn't happened yet.

I'm pretty the sure I made it pretty the clear yesterday that the Felix Box o'Fun and Excitements needs more excitements when it hit the floor and all the not excitements smashed and crashed. I can't be any more clear. What am I supposed to do, draw a picture?

What do I get for my excellent communicationings today? The Felix Box of not Fun or Exciting anymore back in my cage. With mom, looking at me saying "Oh, Felix, I knew you would like your new toys! You are inspired to throw them around and let me pick them up. You are so silly!"

There is no fixing confused.

I throw out the not fun and exciting wrong idea new toys to roll them under dad's chair. Specificallying showing what is not fun or exciting. But the no. No, that is not understandable either. Doghead grabbed one and ran off distracting mom from my point. She is running after doghead yelling, "Drop it! Drop it!"

Angus is running around drooling.
There is no fixing confused.

Mom has run by my cage yelling drop it four times now. Doghead is still drooling. And my point is waiting to be made. How many points do I have to make to get some fun and excitement in this box?

There they go, that's five times now. You know if you watch mom chase doghead she looks like the hobbit running after the Golem.

So. Bored.

So. Not. Fun. Not. Excitements. Bored.

Six! Angus is chasing mom now, they are so confused. Ironicallied when doghead chases mom they still look like the hobbit chasing Golem. This time the Golem isn't drooling as much.

So. Bored.

I'm going to go ahead and throw all the foods out of all the bowls in all the places. Doghead will stop and eat. Mom will stop and give up and look at me to say something ridiculous and I will throw my Felix Box o'Excitements back on the floor to prove my points for one more time.

July 12th, 2019
Presidentialing Rally Speech to the Ralliers.

Grey Strength!

I am Felix R LaFollett and I am running for the Presidentialing of the United States. I am the RIGHT write in candidate!

Today I am here to remind you now that I will always be here fighting The Confused. Alsotoo, I will be here tomorrow trying to help with the not so confused. Which should not be confused, with not confused. Not so confused, is still confused! Grey Strength! Knowing you are not so confused is the first step to becoming not confused.

(Insert hurrahs and hurray's and cheers of HOPE FOR CONFUSED!)

One thing I will make the sure happens is respecting the not confused idea that we all get to choose! Freedom of the choices! You shouldn't choose to be confused, but since there is the freedom of the choices I suppose you could choose to be confused. But then there is no hope. I suggest you don't do that!

(Insert chants of DON'T DO THAT!)

The Grey House of the Presidential Felix will always support your right to keep your flavor, even if there are other flavors to choose from, because FREEDOM OF CHOICE! That's why! If you like your flavor, you can keep your flavor.

The Felix Campaign for the Presidential wants to meet the tracking device and flavor needs of all our supporters and constituents. We choose YOU!

(Insert Yays! and cheers of WE CHOOSE FELIX!)

Today The Felix Campaign for Presidentialing 2020 offers you a NEW flavor and NEW tracking device to add to your trainings! Patriotic Pasta Wheelie! It's delicious! It's nutritious! And your tracking device tells everyone around you that YOU are not confused! Because The FELIX knows where you think you are going!

(Insert cheers and chantings of WE'RE NOT CONFUSED!)

Today I announce the opening of the Official Felix's Snack Attack Emporium on the internets! Your go to it, one stopping to do the not confused shopping, for any theone who chooses NOT CONFUSED!! Alsotoo, of the course all the sales goes to The Oasis Sanctuary and Parrot Retirement Village. By the time I am done fixing all this confused, I will need to retire.

If you want to share your not confused bigger, you can go directlies to my Felix's 2020 Propaganda Campaign Store to get things to stick in your lawn, wear to the office, stick on your clown car, and drink refreshments from while you show you're not confused to the confused and not so confused (but still confused). All propagandas come with internal tracking technologies that upload your location directly to the Felix Satellite Systems in space! Because I know where you think you are going. Even in space!

It is time to share the truth about not confused! You have to choose it! I'm super cereal. Not confused just doesn't jump in your face and say, "HEY! It's me. Now you aren't confused." That's not how any of this works.

(Insert cheers of greatness and exciteables!)

Share your choice so others cannot be confused! I can't do this alone, that would be ridiculous. And exhausting. Grey Strength to Americas. Grey Strength to the Worlds. And Grey Strength to each and every one who is confused, not so confused and now, NOT CONFUSED!

Vote Felix! Vote Not Confused!

Bring Pistachios!
Thank you for my supports!

August 6th, 2019

I see how it is now.

Mom and dad get the stuffed up nose holes but THEY don't go to the doctors to get wrapped in smelly clown towels to get water squirted up their clogged nose holes. ONLY THE FELIX has to do that.

I see how it is now.

Mom and dad get the stuffed up nose holes but THEY just lay around blowing nothings out of their nose holes that don't work, relaxationing. THE FELIX has to go BACK to the doctors to get wrapped in smelly clown towels to get water squirted up my clogged nose holes when THE FELIX has a closed nose holes though. No relaxationing for the FELIX! Doctor grows my nose hole booger trees and won't give them back.

Mom and dad just sit on the couch relaxationing not having to worry about stolen nose hole booger trees in petri dishes that belong to them but got STOLEN. ONLY THE FELIX has to do that.

I see how it is now. Dad eats ice creamers to unplug HIS nose holes. FELIX DOES NOT.

Mom relaxes with her feets up and says ridiculous things like, "OH, I'm sorry, FELIX I can't make the upside downers eggs because I am sick." "OH, I'm SORRY, FELIX I can't play catch toys you throw from Felix's amazing Box o' Excitements because I have a stuffy NOSE HOLE." "OH, I'M SORRY, FELIX that you are so bored because I am sick."

"OH, I'M SORRY, FELIX even though I'm just lying on the couch watching Deadpool movies and blowing my nose holes out waiting to not be sick so I can do the right things for THE FELIX, some day, but NOT TODAY!"

Dad relaxes with his feets down playing the XBoxer shooting aliens and says ridiculous things like, "OH I'M SORRY FELIX I can't scratch your head right now because I am sick." "OH I'm SORRY FELIX I have to drink this drinks that's not a Felix drink. It's a sick dad drink." "OH, I'M SORRY, FELIX I'M STILL SICK so I can't set up your Felix TV Tray of delicious snack attacks and let you help me shoot aliens because I'm sick."

Well, it's a good thing everybody's not sick now. Because I'm so cereal, I almost died of the boreds. Waiting for you to get the betters.

I'm cereal ...I ALMOST DIED OF THE BOREDS!

Do I smell spaghetti saucers?

August 27th, 2019

Mom is distractible. First she's busy. Then she's working. Then after that she's almost done. And then after that that, she's just about there. And then finally she says, okay Felix.

All that is in the wrong order.

My sister is getting weddinged to her fence. I know him. He is not confused at all. Mom is now distracted because of all this weddinged business. Mom says she is now THE notorious M.O.B. I have no the idea what she is saying. I know I am THE Felix and need snacks immediatelies.

When my sister and her fence get weddinged mom will be gone for six days. Which is six SaturDADdays in a row. Which is six pancakes, 40 pistachios, six XBoxer games shooting the aliens with my laser beams, six snack attack movie tabling movies, six dad wake ups with the laughs in the showers and no tsunamis, at the least six beats for the feets guitar jams and alsotoo, extra snacks for the Felix. Because mom forgets extras. Dad does not. Which proves mom is confused and dad is not.

Three days in the rows mom is on the internets making me help her pick her The Notorious M.O.B. dress. Do you like this one Felix? Do you like this color Felix? Felix, what do you think about this dress? Should I wear sparkly shoes!? Not the once did she ask Felix if he wanted the sparkly fizzy drinks with the dipp'n sauce and pretzel stickels. Not. Once. You know there are way too many dresses on the internets. And way too many sparkly shoes I do not care about. I told her grapes are good. She picked a grape dress with grape sparkly shoes to match the grapey.

I'm glad that's over.

Then mom is on the cellphoner with my sister and she's talking about all the dresses and sparkly shoes and how confused she is and that she finally bought a grape dress because The Felix said it was the best idea. My sister said, "What are you saying mom?"

THAT'S WHAT I SAY EVERY DAY!

The tropicaled storm Dorian is coming over here. How annoying. Doghead is scaredy cat about rains and storms. He runs up the stairs and hides under all the blankets and pillows on mom's bed. I suppose I won't have anything to poop on when the tropicaled storm Dorian shows up.

I told the doghead Angus being scaredy cat isn't very Vice Presidentialing. I could lose the electionings if pictures get out on the internets of him hiding under blankets and pillows. It's all fun and the games during the Presidentialing elections until pictures get on the Facebooks and Instagramers. He didn't say much. He just poked his nose inside my cage and tried to lick my leftover snacks.

What a weirdo.

August 28th, 2019

I am sure glad I have you to lean on right the now. Mom is fruit loopering. I think she needs a nap. Or something stronger.

Here I am listening to her read her book out loud. She wrote the book! Why is she reading it to me!? Out loudly. I have the no idea what editing is or why her deadline is my annoying. But here I am hearing her read on and on about a crow named Jack, a rigorous rhinoceros named Gregory, a ox beetle named Hercules and about a millions other creatures I do not even know! She says I am in the book. She says Butters Dactyl is in the book. I am not in that book. I am right here! Butters is over there. Hanging upside down chewing her talons of dactyl fury.

Mom says she has to read it out loud to hear if the words sound good together. She says there are 65,000 words. I told her I don't have time for this.

She needs a nap.

I need yapplepopcorn with the warm peach teas.

There's a toad named Durden who gives the crow named Jack advice. Pffft!

She needs a longer nap.

Who would take advice from a toad. I met one of those outside once. I was minding my own business eating snacks in my RV on my Felix Table of Viewing Things. A toad, not named Durden, hopped on my Felix Table of Viewing Things without asking permission! He didn't even ask if I wanted to view him!

I shot him with my laser beams of death.

He did not die.

That is how uncooperative toads are, and why you don't ask for advice from them.

No one is going to believe anything in this book of hers. They are going to get to the part about Durden Toad and throw her book against a wall. No one has time for this.

August 29th, 2019

I decided to not be annoyed. Now I'm annoyed. I woke up wanting to not be annoyed but here I am listening to the weathering news saying a Hurricane Dorian with three cats is on the way over here.

I do not have time for this. I do not have time for 3 cats, or 4 cats or 5 cats. I do not have time for the Dorian CAT whatever how themany.

I am the busy Presidentialing candidate coming up with not confused plans.

This takes time. And snacks. I have no snacks right now. Just breakfast. I suppose I could eat that first. Breakfast attacks are almost delicious as the snack attacks. But not.

Every time hurricanes show up they have cats. But, I have not seen one cat, ever. Oh! Irma has 4 cats. No she didn't. I didn't even see one.

Oh! Michael has 5 cats! No, he didn't. There were no cats! Why are they talking about cats all the time.

Alsotoo, if there are spaghetti maps, where is the sauce? That's right, there is no sauce. There are squiggly lines all over the maps. My guinea piggles could draw better than that and they don't have a neck to look at the paper.

I saw weirdo neighborling on his roof cutting branches off his tree. What a weirdo! Those are going to grow back. He doesn't even think of that.

I saw another neighbor put a board on their window, and then leave it there. Now he can't see out of his house. What a weirdo! I bet he's in there weirdoing even more than he does because no one can see his super weirdo in action.

I bet all the weirdos with the boards on their windows are super weirdoing right now.

Presidentialing Campaigning in the Hurricane Seasonings is exhausting.

September 6th, 2019

When this Hurricane Seasonings is over, I will breath the sighings of relief. Nobody has the times for this ridiculous.

Good news! Felix Campaign Trail Mix flavorings, Freedom Green Beanies is ready to go! With a new free tracking device. It's a Goats4Votes Tracker. So stylish. Alsotoo, accurate within three tree tops. That's pretty good for a tracking device.

This new Freedom Green Beanies is delicious! There will be no low blood sugars anywhere! Which will leave room to see the confused easier. A good snack fixes just about everything.

I feel good about my campaign building ups. Once this Hurricane Seasonings, Halloweenies, Thanks the Givings and Santa Claus Christmas Thingy is over we can get the goings. This gives me time to get the tracking devices on my supporters and constituents. I know where everyone thinks they're going, but it's good to know where they went first.

Vice Presidentialing Candidate Angus Lee whined too much yesterday about snack attacks for dogheads. "Oh where's MY snack attack? Don't I get a snack attack flavorings with a tracking device? I'm Vice Presidential, I should have that, too!" And then he licked his butt.

Who does that?

Any theway, Angus Bites Snack Attacks is a thingy now. And his tracking device works with my satellites. I have to get that out into the campaign trail mix, alsotoo.

So much to do. So much confused to fix. So many pistachios not in my bowl.

Weirdo neighborling was under his tree pulling the weeds and mumbling to himself, in his underwears. I'm glad there's only one of him.

I can't fix all that weirdo.

September 17th, 2019
Presidentialing Rally of Excitements Speech

It is historicals today that a doghead runs for the Vice Presidentialing. If you think it is historicals that a trainer is running for the Presidentialing, you are wrong. Seven trainers have gone before me. It was a need to know basis. No one needs to know.

BUT to eliminate the confused! I, The Felix, announce my Presidentialing out loud, in your face! And I bring the first doghead for vice Presidentialing with me!

(insert cheers of FELIX FELIX FELIX! ANGUS! AlsoTOO!)

And to make sure you are paying the attentions I bring ANGUS BITES! Because dogheads fall down naturally. It's even worse when they get the low blood sugars! Angus Bites are Cromchy sweet potato crunchies with peanut butter powerdery nom tastings! Which is doghead talk for eat this, you will like it!

(insert cheers of Dogheads are weirdo we like them, alsotoo!)

And to make sure I can track you a Angus VP tracking device is in there, too! Do not let your doghead wear this, I do not want to know what they are doing. I don't want to know what Angus is doing most of the times either. Do not take this personal.

As you are seeing the Felix Administrationings is inclusive! Goats, Dogheads, Ducks! (Because mom has some, I don't have time to argue about this). Cats! Lizards! Guinea Piggles and Buns are welcome to help all trainers fix The Confused that is now more confused than any confused ever in the historicals of time!

(Insert cheers and screams of the excitements here!)

Today we tell confused there is nowhere to hide! Today we come together, except for Weirdo Neighborling, to destroy confused and insert the not confused!

I can not deal with the Weirdo Neighborling right now. Yesterday he dug a hole. Then he just looked in his hole for ever. He just stood next to his hole looking in it talking to his own head. Who does this? I don't even know where to start with that.

(Insert cheers of WHAT A WEIRDO!)

We will remove The Confused, add the not confused and then form the committee to talk about what to do with the weirdos!

(Insert cheers of WEIRDO COMMITTEE WEIRDO COMMITTEE!!)

Thank you for your supports!
Thank you for wearing your tracking device!
I know where you think you are going! Grey Strength!

October 7th, 2019

Well, that was weirdo.

My aunt and uncle and cousins came to visit.

And before that, weirdo neighborling cut down big trees for no reason but to kill trees. Not Weirdo Neighborling on my side, the other Weirdo Neighborling. They are even the more weirdo!

Thankfulies because of the super DadFence of Securities I don't have to watch their weirdo. Until they found weirdos in buckets who went up the tall trees I can see to chop them all down.

I didn't even know there were buckets for weirdos! I didn't know weirdos were allowed to have sharp loud things that kill trees! That seems ridiculous really. When I am elected Presidentialing I will make the Executive Felix Order that says no weirdo can have buckets, sharp loud things, or look at trees. That should fix that.

Mom has been 100 percent not trainable at all for so long now I can't remember the last time I told her to step me up! But now, everyone is gone. The trees are gone. Mom is sad and exhausted and ready to train.

Which is good. This is the longest she has not trained ever. I was wondering if she would wake up one day and stop working at all. Like a robot that runs out of the energy so you have to plug it in the wall for the energies and then you can turn it back on. Dad says that's a hard reboot.

Mom looks like she needs a hard reboot.

I am hearing the presidential is getting mini peach mints for free! No one told me about mini peach mints the last time I ran for the Presidentialing. I have to figure out if they are delicious. If I want them. If doghead would want them. Or if mini peach mints need to go with the goats for the votes! I have to find a mini peach mint first and figure this out.

So much campaign thingys to do.

Alsotoo, I have to figure out how to train my cousins somehow.

The whole time they were here they were telling me to step up and pointing at me. As the if! I am The Felix. Point that trainee finger somewhere else! Alsotoo sit down until I say your name or yell, here!

I have confused cousins.

My aunt only cared about Kirby Lurker. Which is fine. She said I should be wearing a leather jacket and that I am cool like the Fonzi. Firstly, Leather jackets have no pockets for pistachios. Secondlies. Fonzi is cool like The Felix. Whoever the Fonzi is. That name doesn't even sound real.

My aunt is confused and ridiculous.

My uncle didn't bother me but to say hello and goodbye and smile. He would be a great trainee. So much training room to work with. I bet if I had the time when he was here I could have had him getting me warm tea and dipp'n sauce and pretzel stickels whenever I said hey! Here! He had the look of a good trainee that doesn't know anything yet.

My uncle wasn't confused. He did not act ridiculous.

The other Weirdo Neighborlings need to have their roof cut off immediatelies. So they know what that feels like. There are baby homeless squirrels in the front yard with the ducks getting The Felix time and attentions now. Mom says they need her attentionings until they feel at home in our trees that will never get cut down as long as she lives.

I've noticed confused can live a very long time.

Now that all these thingys are not thingys around here any themore I can get back to work training and campaigning. And finding a mini peach mint.

Diary Thingy, you're lucky you are a thingy and not a Trainer. It's exhausting.

October 26th, 2019

Mom is flying away on Tuesday. Dad and I get the vacationings here. Six SaturDADdays in the row. I can regenerate my Felix Energies for the big Presidentialing Campaign and Dad can play his guitars louder. Rock and the Rolls!! I like big beats for my feets. Dactyls sing louder, so there is that, but all in the alls I like the rock n rolls.

I'm not sure what the others are going to do. Doghead will probably lick his butt like the usuals. Kirby Lurker will probably lurk more looking for mom who is not here and will stop over and ask me why, and then I will have to explain that it doesn't matter. What matters is the treats in my feets. And then he will say, "How can you eat when mom is not here?" and then I will say, "Are you confused or something?"

The Horde will probablies complain about the things they always complain about which is every little thing. Cockatiels like the details. The Dactyls will be dactyly. They like dad better any theway.

Mom said Halloweenie will be when she is gone and to not be afraid. The only thing I fear is no Grey in the White House. All this confused is starting to get on my last nerves.

Dad said we are going to ignore the trick or treaters and eat our own treats in the peace. This is why dad needs no training, and I will be on the vacationings all six SaturDADdays.

Weirdo Neighborling will probably be out in the yard again burying things I don't want to know about. When a weirdo waves at you, you know they are burying things. And you could be next if you wave back. Never wave back to a weirdo. Nothing good will be coming from that!

I better get this SaturDADday under the way. Dad is mowing the grasses. I have time to throw the Felix Box o' Excitements on the floor. And if I don't snack after that I bet I have time to water bowl bath and throw all the waters on the floor and whistle the Whistles of Laser Beams in Space. I need to remind Mom of all the things she is going to miss while she is gone being confused somewhere else. OH! I should chew on the window cover thingies, too.

She will want to remember that while she misses me.

October 28th, 2019

Felix is a storyteller at heart. He especially likes spooky stories. Not gory stories, but spooky. He likes Scooby Doo level spooky.

It was dark. It was dark and windy and cold and alsotoo, spooky. So Spooky and creepy.

In the dark something crunched and cracked and munched. But it was not The Felix. The Felix was alone in the dark and cold and alsotoo spooky room. The winds blew and branches scratched on the window where Weirdo Neighborling looked into Felix's house. So spooky and creepy.

The munch munched again. The crunch followed the munch in the dark. What was the munch? What was the crunch? Felix felt the long cold fingers of the Low Blood Sugars crawling into his brains. So spooky and creepy.

Doghead howled the howl of a doghead warnings of the Low Blood Sugars coming. Guinea Piggles wheeking danger! Danger! DANGER! They could feel the cold fingers of the Low Blood Sugars crawling into their brains.

So spooky and creepy.

Then the Felix saw the eyes in the window and heard the munch and crunching. Eyes, orangey and yellow and creepy. Like High Yellow Pellet Ratios with a fuzzy tail. Then the eyes disappeared and doghead howled at the window, and Leonidas bunny thumped in his cage warnings of dark, cold, and Weirdo Squirrel!

The Legend of the Weirdo Squirrel is so creepy. Weirdo Squirrel knows how to open doors. Some have said the Weirdo Squirrel will be the last thing you see when the Low Blood Sugars come because Weirdo Squirrel ate ALL THE PISTACHIOS while you think you are sleeping but you are not because Weirdo Squirrel sat on your head the whole time but you don't even know it until it's too late.

The Felix Laser Beamed and Microwaved but it was too late. The Felix felt around in the darks and the colds to find all the foods bowls empty. Doghead howled, Piggles wheeked, Leonidas thumped, and the Low Blood Sugars looked at Felix.

"It is time, Felix." Said the Low Blood Sugars.

"But there must be something I can eat!" Felix did not want to go yet, he had to throw his phonesbook out of the Felix Tent yet!

"There is one thing you can eat. It waits there, on your snack attack table. Cantaloupe cut long not square."

Felix looked into the eyes of the Low Blood Sugars in the shocks. "I can't eat that! It's not square!"

"Well, there is delicious popcorn leftover in that bowl over there." Low Blood Sugars was becoming frustrated. This happened every time he wanted to do his job and take The Felix to the other side. Why was this parrot so uncooperative? Low Blood Sugars was just doing his job! Reaping and stuff.

"I can't eat the used popcorns! Why would I eat used popcorns! Just take me now. I might as well just die now." The Felix saw the end nearing.

The dark grew darker, the cold got the colder. The wind got winder. Felix saw the end near. Low Blood Sugars did, too.

Suddenlies, Weirdo Squirrel jumped between Low Blood Sugars and the Felix and shouted, "LEAVE IT!"

Felix woke up inside his Box o' Excitements. Empty pistachio shells surrounded him. Doghead's face was licking close to his talons of fury, trying to get empty shells to crunch.

Mom yelled at the doghead, "Leave it!"

Leave it. He almost did. The Felix almost left it permanentlies!

You don't even know how almost the permanentlies.

November 18th, 2019

There comes the times when I must state the obviouslies. Mom is terminally confused. I'm not a doctor. I can't fix this. Six days she has no training and she comes back like a wild Weirdo Neighborling thinking she has the ideas. She does not.

First, doghead escapes under the fence. Mom goes out and puts blocks in front of the fence. Doghead slithers around and over and under her blocks and the fence and escapes. Alsotoo, I did not know a doghead can turn into a furry snake to do that. I am impressed. Mom put more blocks in front of the fence.

So. Confused.

Doghead slithered and then folded himself in the halfs and escaped again! Alsotoo, I did not know a doghead can turn into a furry origami snake. This is interesting.

Mom put more blocks in front of the fence so now the fence looks like someone built a castle, knocked down the castle and then put up a fence that doesn't hold a furry origami snake doghead. Doghead escaped using his super snaky origami doghead skills. Again.

So. Confused.

Dad stayed home on the SaturDADday. We ate the scrambling eggs. Dad used his brain and thought of an anti-furry origami snake doghead fence fix.

So. Not. Confused.

Dad fixed the fence so good doghead just sits in the backyard harumphing about not successfully furry origami snake doghead escaping. I am FeLOLing! Dogheads pout. I did not know this until now.

Secondlies, I am minding my own Felix Business eating the breakfasts when mom screams out the louds! I almost lost a buttfeather! She is yelling the bad words Felix cannot say, but she says any the time she wants.

She sounds ridiculous. Then she is banging and clanging and saying words and screaming more. I almost lost my last nerve!

Doghead is barking and running the round. Mom is laughing and screaming and running arounds. I don't need this. I have the better things to be paying attention to, like weirdo neighborling who will probably kill us all and bury us in his backyard if I do not keep the watch. We could all die!

What is she yelling about? A palmetto bugger. He decided to come into the house and get warm because it is now cold outside. I don't blame him. No one needs cold toes. I guess she killed him though because she was laughing and saying, "(insert bad word) YOU! You (insert bad word)! HAHAHAA!" And then I heard the garbage can lid slap shut and mom danced into the room shaking saying, "EW!! (Insert lots of bad words here, in any order)" Then she giggled and wheezed like a leaky balloon and wheezy leaked, "GAH!"

I do not know what she used to kill the palmetto bugger in the kitchen. I'm pretty the sure I don't want to know. Maybe it was her foot. She could have stomped him like Godziller. Maybe like the King Kong she smashed him with her fists.

She better not have used my SaturDADday Pancaking Spatula.

November 11th, 2019

Mom wrote her book. I am in it. She read to me the chapter about me and I have to say I am very interesting and funny in this book. She read some other chapters about the crow, and about a ground squirrel and a rhinoceros.

She was very excited about her story and her ideas.

"What do you think Felix? A lot of trainees say it's very funny and sweet!"

What does a Trainer do with a trainee this excited about ideas? It was inevitables. "Your ideas are great! Now get them away from me."

This is the five book she puts me in and I don't get one pistachio royalty. Not one. Oh sure, use my Felix Powers and don't pay me.

When you read this book, read the parts about me first. The rest of it is confused words put in the questionable order.

Additionalies, doghead ate a rock outside. Then he came in and borfered it up on the floor under my cage! Mom ran fast to get it but he ate it, again! Then he ran over and borfered it up under the table! Mom ran over there to get it and he slurped it up to barf it up AGAIN!

I do not need this in my life. I almost FeBorfed!

Thank the goodnesses he borfered it up in his box of doghead containments. Mom got it and threw the globbidy slimy rock away. She almost MomBorfed.

Snickers has been laughing all the morning. He just sits there on his tree scratching his eyeball with his talon of fury, laughing. I asked him what's so funny.

"It doesn't matter."

What does a Trainer do with another Trainer this weirdo?

"Okay dactyl. Now get away from me."

I have the Presidentialing Planning to do. I do not have the times for all this distractions.

First, Vote4Goats Trivia Contesting! To win Felix Campaign buttons and bumper the stickers. I think this is a great idea!

Then Make America Grey Again Poster Contesting! To win Make America Grey Again hats.

Then Felix Campaign Rallys for the excitements!

Then I have to write all the platforming ideas so the confused runs for the hills knowing I am coming!

Then all the kinds of Felix Campaign Propaganda items to make sure the words get out! (Not mom's words, my words.)

After the Santa and the Thanksgivings, The Felix Campaigning gets into the full wing!

So you can see how I do not have time for chapters not about me, FeBorfing, or rock borfering dogheads. I just do not have the times!

Alsotoo, I am suspicious of the weirdo neighborling more than the usuals. I am suspecting he is listening to my ideas. Or he is going to kill me.

Probably he's going to kill me, or kidnap Santa Claus.

Holidays are stressfulled.

The 24th of November proved auspicious for Felix. Santa Claus announced his approval, supports and alsotoo, endorsement of The Felix/Angus 2020 ticket.

November 24th, 2019
Presidentialing Campaign Announcement of the Importants.

The Santa Claus has announced his supports for the Felix/Angus ticket for the Presidentialing Candidate!

Thank you Santa Claus! Everyone knows you are truthful, generous and not confused! And I, The Felix, thank you for your HOHOHO Supports!

November 29th, 2019

Tis the Seasonings!

Thanks Givings was delicious. I ate three times plus a bonus rounds. I took seven digest perch naps and fell asleep in my Felix Box 'o Excitements box. My eyeballs didn't want to work. If your eyeballs say no, just don't go. That's what I say.

Doghead had a big buttroast bone. From the pullings of the porks. He was very excited about eating a buttroast bone. Which makes the sense because he is always snorfling his own buttroast. It is probably refreshing to eat a different buttroast. So he ate the buttroast bone. I ate everything delicious. The dactyls ate some delicious, but not all the delicious and Kirby zoomed around stealing everybody else's delicious. Except the Felix. I suppose somewhere in here there is a pile of Kirby stolen snack attacks.

Dad ate delicious. Mom ate some delicious. They drank the bloody marys. Which is ridiculous. I didn't say hello to any Mary and there was no bloody anywhere. Alsotoo, I was not invited to drink that drink. How rude.

After Santa endorsed me for the Presidential I immediatlies warned him of the Weirdo Neighborling's plans.

I told Santa not to visit the Weirdo Neighborling. I also instructioned him that most likely weirdo will try blinky light tricks and put the blow up Santa and reindeers in the front yards to fool Santa. I warned him about the confused being sticky, and getting all over his Santa suit. I also told him I'm pretty sure weirdo murdered the Easter bunny and buried his bunny body in his weirdo backyard.

Weirdo has no chances on murdering and burying the Santa Claus now! If I am elected Presidential I have asked Santa Claus to become the Director of Good Stuff and Fun Things for the Felix Administration. The problem of confused will have no where to hide if we have Christmas parties on the third Thursday of the months. And twice on the Decembers!

There is not enough fun and laughing. Confused hates that. We will fight confused at home. We will fight confused on the streets! We will fight the confused eating TREATS!!

I know this will work. It works here for the Felix. Except when mom walks in the room carrying her bag of confused. I laugh at her and it just stays there with her.

Any theway, in celebrationings of Santa being safe, The Felix running the successful campaigns AND because Thanks Givings was delicious I made a NEW FLAVOR for the Felix Presidentialing Campaign Trail Mix Collection. Which is alot of words to put in your mouth. Holiday Cheers for Felix! I am excitables about the tracking device. Santa and the Felix are on this one. It is great to have the supports of that guy.

He laughs a lot. He is so not confused.

December 2nd, 2019
The Festive Felix Campaign Speech of HOHOHO!

Grey Strength!

(insert cheers of the whoops and hollers here)

Today I woke up knowing what I knew yesterday! Those other guys are all ridiculous!

(insert chants of No More Ridiculous! here)

They are not going to stop being ridiculous. And they will probably end up annoying, confused, wrong and exhausting. Like my Weirdo Neighborling! But in the white house that should be the grey house!

(insert Make America Grey! Make America GREY!! here)

I perch before you this morning to remind all the Trainers, and their trainees that this is the time for the Parrot Party to fly up, rise the up and, alsotoo, WIN! When trainers train every thebody wins!

The Felix Administrationings will put the environments first! You can't cut down trees! Stop that. Are you stupid or confused!? The Felix will help the farmers grow the hemps to make the paper that mom uses to print her books. Which, and I am super cereal here, you need to be careful reading. Her books are her words, and trust the Felix, they are confused!

Any theway.

The Felix Administrationings will alsotoo, make the waters protected. You can't pour poisons in the water! Stop that. Are you stupid or confused?!

Nobody wants that.

Alsotoo, The Felix will make sure all the farmers, the little farmers, not those other guys. They aren't farmers. They are confused. Only the little farmers know how to take care of the things that are important. Like, delicious snacks and treats and the foods. Those other guys make goopy shape things I'm not eating, including yellow pellets. Stop doing that. Are you stupid or confused!?

And so me, The Felix, perches here today knowing confused is always at the bottom of the bowls. And The Felix knows how to throw it all out and start over!

(insert chants of START OVER! Hurray for The FELIX! here)

And remember the goats. Goats4Votes! Felix 2020!

(insert hurrahs and screams of the joys here)

On the Monday Decemberings 9 I will proclaim a week of GOATS4VOTES QUIZ CONTESTING!

I will have super cereal Felix Campaign Propaganda and treats for the feets to give away for prizes to build the excitements!

(insert GOAT QUIZ!! chants of epic happinesses here)

Thank you for my supports!
Grey Strength!
VOTE FELIX!
Those other guys are on Santa's Naughty list!

December 5th, 2019
Presidentialing Campaign Announcement of Importance

Thank you for my supports! The Felix Campaign wins another supports and endorsementals! Thank you Union Presidential Werthers and the Brotherhood of Locomotive Engineers and Piggles[14]!

Vote Felix! Felix is for the peoples, and the piggles, and the unions, and the not confused, and alsotoo, Goats!!

December 19th, 2019

When dealing with the confused, always remember to let the confused leak out slowly, not fastly. If the confused explodes all over it can ruin the dinners and the conversations about not being confused.

Confused is very sticky, it will just get all over every thething.

December 24th, 2019
Correspondence with Santa Claus

Over the years Santa and Felix built a close friendship. Their correspondence reveals an ease of ideas and thoughts. So much so that Santa Claus officially endorsed Felix for President. And often inquired of his life and goings on. Outside of December, Santa has a lot of time on his hands.

Dear Santa Claus,

Thank you for my endorsements for the Presidential. AlsoToo, thank you for the following things I want for the Christmas that I am sure you will remember to give me because you are the Santa and I am The Felix.

---

[14] Werthers Guinea Pig (piggles being the plural and including Basil Exposition) is the Union President of the Brotherhood of Locomotive Engineers and Piggles having been unanimously voted such by Basil Exposition four years prior. Basil didn't want the job.

1) A new Blue Cup. Snickers Dactyl chewed mine up.

2) A new hangy toy thingy. Snickers Dactyl chewed mine up.

3) A new throwing and chewing box of the cardboards to chew and throw. Doghead stole mine and then chewed it up.

4) A Jail Box with bars and a lock so I can lock up the toothbrush holder and his criminaling gang including toothbrush and lotion squirter. I arrest them and arrest them and arrest them, and then they show up standing in the row the next day laughing at my authority.

5) A not confused brain, for mom. I am exhausted.

6) Two new spatulas for SaturDADday, for dad. To make the things easy for him.

7) A Felix sized water squirter bottle, or water squirter gun with the unlimited rapid firing stream of justice. For doghead. I suppose I can keep using my water bowl, but then I can't take a water bowl bath after it lands on doghead. You can see the problem here I am sure.

8) Earhole plugs. Because, so many reasons.

9) A big red flag with big white letters that spell "OVER THE HERE", with a big white arrow pointing. So I can wave this flag when mom pretends she cannot hear my ambulance-dog barking-back up the truck-laser beam taxi whistling.

10) A new Felix Couch and Blanket. Doghead stole my Felix Couch. Dactyls infested my blanket with Dactyl Cooties.

11) Pistachios. This goes without the explanationings.

12) One rubber band, four straws, seven flipper flopper shoes, and a spork. I have the plans.

13) Pistachios just in the case you forgot number 11.

Be careful riding the sleigh in the sky with your reindeer. Do NOT fall for all those blinky lights and blow up Santa traps in Weirdo Neighborlings front yard. I am pretty the sure the Easter Bunny is dead and buried under his Weirdo Shed of Weirdness in the backyard. Be careful! I would just drop what you have for weirdo in his pool as you fly over to land on the Felix Roof. I told dad to put his super dad ladder of upping on the side of the house and leave the windows open for you. Right next to my cage and tree tent.

Alsotoo, remember to not forget the pistachios. You should probablies use the yellow highlighter pen on Number 11.

Merry the Christmas Santa Claus.
Felix

January 14th, 2020
Presidentialing Campaign Important Announcement

The BATMAN endorses Felix for the 2020 Presidentialing Campaign! Gotham's son rarely involves himself in politics, but this year, under the circumstances of complete confused, the Dark Knight came forward to endorse Felix R. LaFollett. Because those other guys are criminally confused. And BATMAN is on his last nerve.

Confused has nowhere to go. The Batman has grapplinger hooks, and super cereal projectiling nets, and flying batplanes, and batputers, and a cave! I have a tent! We are practicaling twins!

Vote FELIX! #Felix2020 #BATMANEndorsements

Thank you for my endorsement for the Presidential The BATMAN. It is super cereal exciting to know that when the crime fighter thinks of fighting the crimes he endorses The Felix! Because The Confused will be arrested during a Felix Presidentialing Administrationing. I am not messing the arounds.

Thank you for my supports! Thank you for Voting the Felix!

Together I know where you think you are going!

January 16th, 2020

Square is square and round is round and that other shape is wrong. That other shape that is not square is always wrong and I told mom it was wrong the first day I threw all the cantaloupies on the floor. What part of Door Knocking-Dog Whistle-Back Up The Truck-Seagull Yelling doesn't she understand?

Here I am, supervisoring her chopping and cutting and what do I get? The other shape not square. I suppose a round cantaloupie would make the untrained trainee think that all the parts inside are round, if they think alone. Which she is doing with me in the room. I told her a long time ago do not think alone, I am here! Just don't do it. What part of Head Spin Shake-Water Bowl Dump-Food Toss-Wing Flap-Old Grumpy Guy Growl doesn't she understand. I made myself very clear.

Here I sit full of round cantaloupies. I had no choice. It was the low blood sugars dying or eating round cantaloupies. I will probably end up with the indigestionings and refluxors.

AlsoToo, speaking of the indigestionings. Did you see what the Kirby did to The Felix yesterday?

I was ready to deliver my Epic Speech of The Felix. He was supposed to stay upstairs and throw everything in the sink. But noooo, Kirby shows up and takes over my video time and speech. Mom just shrugged and smiled. You can't be more confused than that.

This is exactlies why I fired the Kirby and asked Angus Doghead to be my Vice Presidential Runnermate. Because all you have to do is sit, stay, and roll over when you are Vice Presidenting. Just sit, pant a lot if you have to, but sit.

I have to get mom in line. She's delirious and unstabled. First thing after lunch I am throwing everything out of my Box o'Excitements. Then I will throw the Box o'Excitements on the floor. Explode my phonesbook, on the floor. Throw all the dactyl foods on my Felix Weirdo Neighborling Observatory, on the floor. Take a water bowl bath, and throw all the water on the floor. Fly nine times to the stairs when she thinks she is thinking. I can have a word with her during Taxi Service back to my cage. Which I will then make sure to say, Crow Calling-Dog Barking-Ambulance-Back Up The Truck-Laserbeam-Bomb Drop Explosion-Door Knocking-Head Spinner.

If she can't understand that, I will have to train all the way back to the beginning. How annoying.

February 11th, 2020
Presidentialing Campaign Rally Speeches of the Rally

Hail and Grey Strength to you!

I perch before you today to share my story of The Felix!

(Insert cheers and gasps of the excitements here)

Some of you may not know why I know where you think you are going. Some of you may not know why you are thinking alone. And some more of you may be not thinking at all but stuck standing in a room thinking, "how did I get here any theway?"

A long time ago I was just Felix. Everybody called me Franklin, because they were confused and not going anywhere. Then I rescued mom and dad to make sure at least two trainees would have some hope of a not confused life. Remember you can't save everything or every the one, but you can be everything to that one confused you saved.

I struggled. I fought the low blood sugars, the name Franklin, the wrong bedtimes, almonds instead of pistachios! I faced the insurmountables of wrong side up broccolis! But I did not give the ups!

(Insert FIGHT FIGHT FIGHT!!!! The Strugglings are real! here)

Remember this one thing of the confused, it will change every other thing if you remember this one thing. There are no teams! There is us, and there is confused and that is it. It is like watching the footballing games. Two teams fighting, and some sit in chairs to root for one team. And some sit in chairs to rally for the other team. And all the times you are rooting for teams that don't even know you or where you think you are going, there is somebody sneaking behind you and stealing TREATS FROM YOUR SEATS!! Why? Because you are too busy cheering for confused teams that do not know about you at the all!

(Insert boos and the hisses NO MORE CONFUSED here)

Thank you.

I know. You know. They know. But the important thingy is now you know the real thing that they don't want you to know! Which is all of them, all of those other guys are so confused they forgot they are confused!

(Insert THIS IS RIDICULOUS! WE NEED THE FELIX! here)

As your Presidentialing Candidate I am here today to make sure you know the stuffs that need knowing. So you can forget the stuffs that don't need knowing and wake up tomorrow the morning knowing even the more; they are the confused, not us!

When in doubt about the confused you see or hear just ask the questioning; Would Felix say that?

(Insert chants FELIX WOULD, THEY WISH THEY COULD!)

We move the forward today together knowing there are no teams, just thingys that have to get done. Like Universal Goats! Alsotoo, no low blood sugars for any thebody! I'm cereal. If you get sick, you get help quick! Today we say no more teams and no more hiding behind the hooplas and the badwordings!

(Insert hurrahs and happys for being the nice!)

Today with the Felix Campaigning you know Universal Nice and Not Confused is where we are going! That's where you thought you were going. You were just following the wrong guys.

(Insert cheers of FOLLOW FELIX! HE KNOWS WHERE WE THOUGHT WE WERE GOING! NO MORE CONFUSED!)

Thank you for my supports!

Join me today, fight the confused tomorrow, take the nap the next day!

(insert jumpings and up the down screamings of exciteables and energizing!)

I am Felix R. LaFollett and I am running for the Presidential. Alsotoo, I approve this message and any other message I say because, I am The Felix.

February 20th, 2020

Just before the Pandemic hit hard, and shut things down Felix held his first public Rally of 7 planned. The Rally was a huge success empowering Felix and his attitude and confidence. Although that never really wains, but you know, you can't have too much Felix Attitude, according to Felix.

Campaign Rallying went the pretty well. Every body had a seat and then some bodies stood up in the back and on the side of things. Every body got a tracking device. And some bodies bought my book to help their confused. Which is pretty the good.

Mom had to talk and try to convince the bodies that she was not confused. Of the course I know she is permanently stuck. When I was waiting for her to stop trying, a dove landed on a net over my head. I told him that net was for Trainers. And that the Rally for was trainees. And that looking up at his buttfeathers was awkward.

Jerry the Dove told me he was just taking the rest from the cold outside and that he liked eating Trainer foods and there was always some for him to find in the parrot store.
Which I suppose made some senses.

He asked what mom was talking about. I told him it didn't matter.

He asked what I was going to do if she stopped. I told him most the likely try to help the bodies in the chairs get tracking devices.

He asked why I wanted to track the bodies. I asked him wouldn't he feel better knowing where every the body thought they were going before they got there. Jerry was impressed with my plans.

Alsotoo, there was chanting of "Felix! Felix! Felix!" That was musicals to my earholes. The confused is on the run!

I almost starved though. I only had one foods bowl and one drinking bowl and not one pistachio the whole time. Mom said it was only one hour. I'm pretty sure it was four days.

Dad recorded the whole rally on the video thingy. I will make sure it gets up on FelixTV and you will see first hands how out of the controls mom can get when she thinks by herself in front of other trainees.

March 3rd, 2020

On the 3rd of March everything changed. Changed in ways that are still revealing results no one can predict. Yet. Dad's company sent everyone home to work. Stores closed. Sheltering in place became a thing. The world as we knew it, stood still as citizens of the world faced a pandemic. Awkwardly. Poorly. Stubbornly. Ridiculously.

Inside the chaos of no action, reaction, and poorly planned actions 2020 unfolded itself as one big global Shakespearean tragedy.

Humor in corners existed to help move things along.

Felix took his role as a light hearted, but serious Presidentialing Candidate forward without rallies, but with the sincerity only a parrot can muster with one last nerve ending.

Greyt news! Dad is working from the home because of the Cry'noutloud Virus Thingy. Everyday is now SaturDADday! Un thefortunetlies pancakes are not included in the dealings. He says he has to work. I say making pancakes IS the important work.

Mom is here as usuals. Which means the forces of confused and not confused are fighting it out. So far the confused is winning because dad does not have the spatula.

I reminded him that pancakes have vitamins and the minerals to fight the Cry'noutloud Virus Thingy. Alsotoo, the energies. He did not pick up the spatula. Mom did and I told her to put it down. I hate panslurpies.

I am excitables about the coming soon new Campaign Trail Mix Flavor for the Felix Campaign. Two new tracking devices, and two new flavors packed into one with a special extra tracking device. Fighting confused requires treats and tracking devices. That's scientifical.

Speaking of the scientifical, if pancakes have vitamins and the minerals and there is a spatula, make pancakes. Follow the science to pancakes.

If you can't find the pancakes, campaign trail mix delivers the flavors to savor and the nutritionals, without the spatula. My campaign cooker chef is putting lots of nutritionals into the the Mini Peach Mints and Applequital Bits. When in doubt, treat your Cry'noutloud Virus Thingy! Keep the tracks of campaign flavors to savor is what I say.

Dad just walked by, he did not have a spatula. Someone should invent pancake vitamins. Pancake vitamins that are little teeny vitamins that fit in your face and deliver the flavor to savor with the vitamins you don't taste. You just taste pancakes. That would be greyt.

Dogheads just wrestled into my tree stand tent. There is no cure for them.

Then the Cry'noutloud Denim Pants Virus Thingy showed up and I started Sheltering in my face.

This is going to get so weirdo.

March 14th, 2020

Today is day number a million of the shelter in my face. Dad is home working from the shelter in my face. Which is the good thing. It's SaturDADdays until the Cry'noutloud Virus Thingy stops whatever it is doing that makes trainees confused about finding toilet papers, hiding toilet papers and yelling about toilet papers. Which I don't have to worry about. I do not have the butt cheeks. I have the floof opening.

Any theway, Dante DuBois Doghead is distracting Angus Lee Doghead, my Vice Presidentialing campaign partner. He is not taking the campaign trail cereal. Except when he gets the Campaign Trail Mix. He still sits, stays, and rolls over though. Most times they chew each other's head.

Yesterday dad made the breakfasts and didn't share. Today dad made the eggs and bacons. I got the eggs, not the bacons. None of this is working out. I should get the bacons. These are the ending times! I do not want to be dying of the low blood sugars and the Cry'noutloud Virus Thingy and thinking, "I could have had the bacons ..."

Tomorrow is another day of sheltering in my face. I hope dad realizes pancakes are scientifically proved to kill the low blood sugars. All the scientists say, "Oh yes, pancakes are very scientifical. You should feed The Felix right away!" I heard them myself.

I have new toys in the Box o' Excitements. Someone should invent bacon toys.

Mom is taking the Angus Lee on a doghead walk. Dante DuBois is a puppy doghead and can't keep up so he stays here and snorfles his butt. Maybe there's bacon in there. I don't know.

The Zon Guy brought a box to the door. Mom said she is fulfilled. And that there is all the doghead poop bags dogheads need for 25 years. What is the deals with Cry'noutloud Virus Thingy making every one worry about pooping!?

If I get bacons with my pancakes tomorrow that will be great. It will make up for the million days of shelter in my face and the Weirdo Neighborling banging in his backyard. He sounds like a woodpecker that's a hundred feet tall.

Wait.

What if it IS a hundred feet tall woodpecker?

If you have a fistful of treats in the one fist, and a fist full of treats in the other fist you fall off a digesting perch. This is science. It is called Physics. Snickers does not believe in Phystics. He is laying on his back two talonsfuls of treats feet, at the bottom of his cage.

He's not even embarrassed about that.

March 24th, 2020
Presidentialing Campaign Sheltering in my Face Rally
Speech over the internets

Grey Strength!

It is day million and two more of the Cry'noutloud Virus sheltering in the face. It is also annoying. Today will live in the inseams! Because today we the peoples of the world and other places say, "Hey! Are we done yet I am bored in here!"

As your Presidential Parrot Party Candidate I am here to tell you in there, I know where you thought you were going, but you're going to have to wait. Alsotoo, continue to wear your tracking devices. In case you think you are going anywhere anyway.

Do not have the worries though. When I am Presidential the first thing that will happen to fix this is get rid of The Confused. I'm cereal. It is easy to get confused by the emergencies that feel like emergencies but they are just confused. I will make the sure there are tests! No math test though. I hate those.

Alsotoo, not tests that ask a lot of questions either. There is no time for a lot of questions!

As your Presidential I will make the sure everyone gets the masks. They will be BATMAN masks! BATMAN fights confused all the times. Once I saw Batman fight a bad guy that told jokes. He beat him with the grappling hook and also some bat throwing thingys. As Presidential I will make the sure there are BATMAN masks, grappling hooks and bat throwing thingys to fight The Confused Cry'noutloud Virus Thingy!

(INSERT CHANTS OF I AM BORED IN HERE!!)

In the Felix Administrations I will have scientists all over the place!

(INSERT HURRAHS OF SCIENCE! SCIENCE! SCIENCE!!)

As you know, science says pancakes fight the low blood sugars. Not having the low blood sugars fights the Cry'noutloud Virus Thingy! I will appoint the Chief Scientist of Pancakes in my first 100 minutes!

(Insert chants of PANCAKES PANCAKES PANCAKES! WHAT ABOUT THE BACONS!?!?)

And the bacons!!!!

(INSERT THE SCREAMS OF THE JOYS OF BACONS TOO! BACONS TOO! BACONS TOO!!!)

For the now we must focus on today, here not the tomorrow over there. Sit down. Take the naps. Make sure all your Trainers have treats for their feets. Make the sure your Trainer is not bored and alsotoo has all the treats needed for the sheltering in the face. Wear your tracking device for safety. Sit down.

For me, and my Vice Presidentialing candidate runnermate, we will keep the keeping on to win the Presidential so that confused will finally be wiped out forever!

(INSERT CHANTS OF WE ARE OVER IT! FELIX FELIX!)

In the fight against the confused I have asked my Chief Treats Scientist to make a new flavor to savor for the Campaign Trail Mix!

It is filled with delicious nutritious anti Cry'noutloud Virus beating up vitamins!

Mini Peach Mints with Applequittal Bits! That's right! And two new tracking devices to choose from and wear where you think you are not even going to go yet! And because I know how to Presidentially think! There is a Get Out Of Jail FREE card with the coupon for more treats for your Trainer's feets later! If criminal activities pays the other guys, then it will pay us alsotoo!

(INSERT CHEERS VITAMINS TO WIN! FAIR IS FAIR!!)

Thank you for your time. I know you have a lot of it right now sitting over there. I have just enough time to stop mom from walking into another wall. Grey Strength! Thank you for my supports! Vote Felix! Stop the confused! Take the nap! Eat the Treats! Kiss the beaks and listen to your Personal Trainer!

Together we will beat the confused! And get out the sheltering. So Ridiculous. Watching Weirdo Neighborling shelter in the face is awkward.

Thank you for my supports! I am Felix R LaFollett and I am running for the Presidential!

Grey Strength!

March 27th, 2020

Today is the million and whatever, I'm not going to count anymore cry'noutloud shelter in my face.

Dogheads are wrastle wrestling so the much Dante Doghead is now limpy. Angus Doghead is lumpy and mom is saying the things, like "In your kennel."

"Time out."
"Stop."
"Wait."
"Stop chewing his head."
"Get out of the bathroom."
"Get off the table."
"Why are you doing that?"
"What are you doing?"
"Where are you?"
"Stop snuffling that!"

She has lost the total controls. I warned her, but the no. Don't listen to the Felix, go ahead and get more confused. There isn't enough of that around here.

I'm sheltering my face in the Felix Tree Tent. I'm not looking at any of that.

Snickers Dactyl has decided that he wants mom to yell at him. "What are you doing?"

"Stop chewing on the window."
"Where do you think you are going?"
"Get off the floor."
"Step up. Not there. Here."
"Leave the doghead alone."
"Doghead, leave the dactyl alone."
"What is going on?"
"Stop throwing the foods."

-Which I don't care about because that's not my foods any theway. -

"What are you yelling at?"
"Is that yours?"
"That's not yours."

She has lost the total controls. I warned her, but the no. Don't listen to the Felix, go ahead and let a dactyl run around. See where that confused gets you.

The ConfusedTV is on again today. I do not recommend the ConfusedTV. Once you hear the news of the news, turn it off. Maybe turn on FelixTV. Or maybe no TV and train with your Trainer. The silver liner is Training Can Commence. There's nothing else to do but train. Binge train instead of the binge watch. Read my training book. Read your Trainer's mind. Confused is simmering all over the place waiting for everyone to come back out of the shelter in the face and then WaBLAMMO! We have to start all over again. There is no time for starting all over again. It's time to get the ship shaped for the Felix Campaign. There is confused every thewhere.

Last time I saw this much confused some guy in a store called me Franklin and said I was for the consignment sale!

GAH!

Any theway, Weirdo Neighborling is sheltering on his roof with the blower of his leaves. Who does that?

Maybe he ran out of things to blow around inside his weirdo house.

April 10th, 2020

Today is one trillioning four hundred thousand million days of the Cry'noutloud sheltering in my face. I'm only counting because I am bored.

Mom is getting twitchy.

Dad is not twitchy, but he is not making the pancakes. It is too early to say he is confused. He is symptoming confused things though. Mom being twitchy, and dad now being almost confused, I am pretty sure the contaminationings are going back and forth. They keep kissing. This is not helping me. How am I supposed to train them if they are twitchy and contaminated with the almost confused.

The problem with almost confused is the almost confused don't know they are. Because they are almost not confused, at the same time. So they let their almost not confused brain side tell their almost confused brain side, that it is wrong. And since they are on the verging of full confused, well you can see the brain fart coming. And then mom is twitchy, alsotoo. Nothing good can come from this. Especially the pancakes.

Dogheads are still chewing on each other's faces. There is no hope for them.

Weirdo Neighborling comes outside into my viewings. He needs to shelter in his own face in his own place. I should not have to look at all of that confused I can't fix from here. His Weirdo Doghead meets my dogheads at the fence. Then they all pee on the fence at the same time. WHO DOES THIS!?!? Mom says they are arguing about who owns the fence.

Who argues about a fence that is covered in pee? WHO DOES THIS!?

Neighborlings across the street started feeding mom's ducks. I keep telling her they are not her ducks. They are their own ducks and they can do what they want.

Now she is trying to feed them things that are better than the neighbor foods.

It is a duck feeding food contest. I need to find a trainee to get mom to have a Felix Feeding Food Contest. Alsotoo, this is not the Weirdo Neighborling, this is the not so Weirdo Neighborling that lives where my windowing is not. So, the weirdo is very low.

Any theway, my rabbit friend, Leonidas is thumping a lot since the sheltering in my face. He says since mom and dad are here both, he should be getting two times the foods. Rabbits are fast with math. And they always make the sense.

There is going to be a lot of the confused work to do after the sheltering in my face. The Parrot Party Campaign is running smooth, and tracking devices are indicating a surge against the confused. And the annoying. And the ridiculous. If you have to sit still long enough, to listen long enough, and then have to live with what the confused just did to you. You get annoyed. I know. A guy called me Franklin once. He thought he was doing me the favor.

We are surrounded by confused. It probablies feels like it is closing in on us like a smelly burrito doctor towel. BUT! I say, ahHA! Confused! The jokes are on you! We will vote you out and vote in the Parrot Party of NOT CONFUSED!

April 15th, 2020

A duck decided to walk back and the forth outside on top of the outside roof. Back and forth and back and forth. Ducks have big flat feets that thud. Angus Doghead says, "I'll get it!" and barks and jumps up and tries to climb the house to the roof. Without the Dad Ladder.

Mom says, "Stop!"
Dad says, "Angus knock it off!"
Angus Doghead says, "I can get it!"

Now, it's mom and dad and Angus Doghead going back and forth.

Duck doesn't care, though. I hear his thuddy stomps back and forthing. Dad should just tell Angus Doghead he can't climb walls. He is not the spider or the lizard. He can't fly. He is not the Felix. He can't climb trees. He is not the twitchy squirrel.

He is a confused doghead that can only snortle snorfles his butt. And not even his own butt! I saw him snortle Dante Doghead's butt! And Donte Doghead let him. And then Dante Doghead chomped on Angus Doghead's face. And then Angus Doghead chomped on Dante Doghead's face.

Then mom said, "STOP!"
Dad said, "ANGUS KNOCK IT OFF!"
Angus Doghead said, "WHAT?"
Dante Doghead said, "IT WASN'T ME!"

It wasn't, it was Dante Doghead's butt being snortle snorfled. But hey, don't ask the Felix. What do I know? Only everything.

Any theway, mom said she had four gooey bananas to make the banana bread. I told her that I would like to go outside in my RV so I am ready for the house to burn down. I don't even want to know what banana bread slurpies taste like. It's probablies like panslurpies but with banana burnt insides.

May 12th, 2020

Cry'noutloud Virus Thingy is on my last nerves. It's the one thing for toilet papers to disappear because I do not have the butt cheeks. It is another thing for the pistachios to disappear because of the hoarders who are not me. Alsotoo, you can not wipe your butt cheeks with pistachios so what is up with that?

Mom said not to worry. She also said she knows what she's doing. There's no point in letting her know she doesn't and I do. She gave me the walnut and said hang in there Felix. I am not a bat.

Dogheads are now even more weirdo. Angus Doghead pulls the Felix Blanket of Comfortings off the Felix Couch and then Dante Doghead gets on my blanket, and then Angus Doghead gives him rides around the house. Did I mention all that stuff is mine? Except the dogheads. I don't want any of that annoying.

Mom tries to pick Dante Doghead up off my blanket and says, "GAH! My back! You are a hippo!"

There is no point in letting her know doghead is not a hippo.

Then she grabs Angus Doghead's doghead necklace and says, "You look like a stupid pony!" And kisses his head.

There is no point in letting her know Doghead is not a stupid pony. Alsotoo, if he was, why would you kiss a stupid pony on the head?

Then Angus Doghead wags his butt rope and starts pulling Dante Doghead again.

Then she tells Angus Doghead to sit. And then she says, "NOT ON DANTE'S HEAD!"

This part is hilarious. I don't say anything.

Did I mention all that stuff is mine?

I had a dream last night that I lived in a building of lots of trainees who are in the college doing college thingys. I was trying to take a nap and every minute a colleger came in and said confused things and asked confused questions. I shot them with my Laser Beam PEWPEW! and said, "GET OUT OF MY ROOM, STUPID PONY!"

They exploded into phonebooks.

You can see my last nerves are exposing.

May 13th, 2020

I am still sheltering in my face. I was dreaming the dreams and woke up forgetting. Then I saw Weirdo Neighborling sheltering in my face in his backyard. All of his weirdo just hanging out there. I do not need all that all hanging out over there.

Leonidas rabbit played the tricks on Dante Doghead when I was eating breakfast not looking at all that weirdoing. Dante stuck his head inside Leonidas Condo to snortle a bunny butt. Leonidas kicked him in the face. I laughed so hard I lost a buttfeather.

Dogheads make the best faces of annoyed when a rabbit kicks them in the face.

BAHAHAA! *fartsound*

Dad is doing the meetings on the laptopper. Something about research and tags and uploading the datas and downloading the datas and something else about Todd being slow and every thebody on the laptopper laughed and laughed. Except Todd.

He laughed and then said something about every thebody shutting the h-e-double-helicopter up. And then every thebody laughed on the laptopper.

Now I know what dad does when he "goes to the work to make sure Felix has enough pistachios always". He laughs on laptoppers.

Sheltering in my face has made the things pretty clear. Dogheads don't care about it. Rabbits only care about dogheads snortling and snorfling their rabbit butts. Dad is pretty the funny on a laptopper. Mom is confused with or without pandemics. Pistachios can run out. Weirdo Neighborlings are really really good at sheltering in the face. I think they like knowing they can weirdo because no one is around. And so they weirdo extra.

Dad told mom the new window blinders are coming soon. Which is good. I need my window to be blind until Weirdo is done hanging all his weirdo out there.

May 18th, 2020

SaturDADday was the fantastics! First, dad. You know what that means. Seconds, I have a Guardian Pistachios Angel! Who the knew!? GPA sent me the pistachios, for me. GPA didn't say share any thewhere at all. GPA wrote me the notes to read to Mom about not sharing.

Thank you Guardian Pistachio Angel! I am safe and secures because of you.

Alsotoo, these are delicious! Way thebetter than what mom gets. I told her to go ahead and get these from now on. Because a GPA knows what's best about the best pistachios.

Guardian Pistachios Angels. I am still energizing from knowing this now!

Today we are getting the tornadoes. And the rains. And the winds. And the lightenings. The sun left because it hates tornadoes. Mom says this is fine by her since now she doesn't have to pay the electrical company as much money. She is so confused. The sun isn't a lightbulb. I am going to have to break the news to her that the sun is not plugged in around here. It's ginormously huge floating in the spaces, a ball of gasses on fire. In the sky. Even if you could plug it in for the backups, I bet there isn't the extensioning cord long enough to reach.

And you probably have to have a surging protector, too. Mom has the no ideas about these things.

Angus Doghead hates the stormage. He is hiding under beds, under blankets on beds, under pillows and under piggle cages. Trotting around the house looking for hiding spots. I hate to break the news to him but tornadoes aren't looking for him any theway. He is wasting his times. Tornadoes look for barns to suck up into the sky and drop.

I saw that on a movie. I saw a cow get sucked up, and a house, and a girl in the house and she was yelling about her Auntie M&Ms. Then the tornado dropped the girl and the house on the wicked witch of easts. And then the wicked witch of the wests showed up smoking and yelling and pointing green fingers at the girl. And then goodness witch showed up and told her to be gone. And she did. Kind of. Things got weirdo after that.

I doubt flying monkeys are real. If they were they would get out of the zoo all the times.

I saw a video of a zoo full of penguins visiting fish aquariums. A whale said hello to the penguin. The penguin said to the other penguin, "What the H E double helicopter is THAT!?!"

The cameras guy didn't hear that. The penguin whispered it. I can read penguin lips. The whale got offended because he could read penguin lips.

The camera guy didn't even know they argued for 3 minutes before the penguins walked away harrumphing. It seems to the Felix if you are going to camera penguins, you better know how to read their lips. He missed all the good parts.

Sheltering in the face leaves lots of the times to watch videos of weirdo things. And bad camera guy works.

Thankfullies, thanks to my Guardian Pistachio Angel, I won't get the low blood sugars!

The tornadoes just ended. I suppose Weirdo Neighborling will have to come out and shelter in my face.

May 19th, 2020

Mom is going essentialing, I have to make the List of the Felix Essentials for not Getting the Low Blood Sugars and things I want anyway. I can't talk right now.

1) New Spatula.

2) Not pistachios. (Remember? I have a Guardian Pistachio Angel.)

3) Pretzel Stickles. (Not the round ones. Not the bendy round ones. Not the chunky ones. Not the broken chunky ones. The stickle ones.)

3) Dipp'n Sauce. (The carrot hummus, not the cauliflower hummus. Who thought of that idea any theway?)

4) Cantaloupies. (The good ones. Not the bad ones. And alsotoo, maybe the yellow ones that are mushy. But don't forget the orange ones no matter thewhats.)

5) Chop sticks. (Bambooy ones with the thingy on the end that is square so I can chew that off.)

6) Baby sippy cup. (A blue top, not a pink top. Alsotoo, not the one with pictures on the side of balloons.)

7) Walnut in half. (Make sure they fit in the blue top sippy cup with no pictures of balloons.)

8) Yogurts. (Not the banana yogurts. The regular yogurts that taste like yogurts.)

9) Apples. (The red ones that are delicious. Not the ones that are not red and delicious. I can't eat those. They give me the burples.)

10) Teeny Tiny paper cups. (Make sure the Pretzel Stickles fit with a walnut.)

11) Paper Towels. (You can have the towels. I want the tuber for later to shred into the bits of tubes to drop on doghead heads. They don't even know I'm doing it. They just walk around with shredded tubers on their head! Hilarious!)

12) A book. How to Make Pancakes not Panslurpies. (That's for you.)

13) Weirdo Neighborling Repellent. (Probably in the bug spray aisle. If it has pistachio scent, get that one. Alsotoo, get the giant economy big bottle.)

14) Squirt bottle that fits my talons of fury. (So I can squirt Dante Doghead. Next time he tries to snortle my Talons. Why you picked a Weirdo Doghead is beyond me.)

15) Pears. (I might or might not eat them. Chopped in little squares, next to my apples chops but not touching. Maybe. Better get them in thecase I feel good about eating that.)

May 20, 2020

SaturDADday trimmed the trees in the front yard where the squirrels come from. My window is not the front yard but the Weirdo Neighborling side fence yard. I know the squirrels come from the front yard because they run by on the fence top yelling, "TO THE BACK YARD!" So obviouslies, they are coming from the other way.

Trees are trimmered higher, the squirrels are running by my window more yelling, "TO THE BACK YARD MORE!"

Annoying. Disturbing. Screaming squirrels get under my fluff feathers. One squirrel stopped right in front of my window and looked in my house! He had beady criminaling activity eyeballs. I shot him with my laser beam PEWPEW! He whipped his fluffy tail at me. I shot him again. He whipped his tail again and yelled insulting things in my face!

Only a squirrel would yell, "YOU IN THE HOUSE! OPEN THE DOOR! BRING US YOUR NUTS!"

I'm pretty sure I can't get mom out there though.

"SQUIRREL!" I said, "I can't get mom to come out, she's nuts, but I can't get her to go outside right now!"

"DO NOT GIVE US EXCUSES BIRD! BRING US YOUR NUTS! WALNUTS! PECANS! PISTACHIOS! DO IT NOW!"

Pistachios? Did that squirrel demand my pistachios!?! You can only push a Felix so far. I yelled, "SQUIRREL!" to Angus Doghead. He jumped up on the Felix Couch and barked and hopped and begged to go out the door. Mom said, "ANGUS! What is your problem? You need to go out AGAIN!?"

She opened the door.

Angus Doghead turned into Angus Cannonball shooting around to my window Weirdo Neighborling fence side and jumped WAY up and almost got that screaming squirrel. So. Close.

Screaming squirrel jumped 43 feet in the airs and climbed to the top of his annoying screaming squirrel tree.

Mess with the Felix you get the doghead. The big one. Not the little one.

It is good to know one of the doghead is more than a butt snortling snorfler.

May 21, 2020

The TV news says mentaling health is important and sheltering in your face does not help. Obviouslies Mister TV Newscaster has met the dogheads personally.

Leonidas Rabbit told me at the breakfast that Dante Doghead stole his toy right from his Condo. Right in front of his face. Not his favorite toy. Not his second favorite toy. But the toy mom got thinking alone, and wasn't a good toy so he kicked it in the corner to keep it. He doesn't want to hurt mom's feelings. Rabbits are very sensativical about feelings.

I said, "I don't know about all that. I just murder the toys she thinks I wanted when I never asked. Then I throw the dead things out of my cage and onto the floors. Or doghead heads. Or in my water bowls. Once I threw a dead thing and it landed on the ceiling fan spinner. Mom turned on the fan spinner and it shot out and into a bowl of her popcorns. Which is what you get when you don't share."

I could see Rabbit was intrigueled by my story. "I would have had time to warn her about the dead thing on top of the ceiling fan spinner while she put the popcorns in my bowls. But after the dead thing ended up throwing her popcorns on the floor she was too busy trying to sweep popcorns between doghead faces eating popcorns. I couldn't get the word in the edgewise."

Rabbit didn't say anything. His face was full of banana.

Dogheads get 10 minutes to doghead wrestle twice the day. In the house. Mom says it's important for the dogheads.

Leonidas Rabbit thumps for 11 minutes when they wrestle. I asked him why 11 and not the 10. He said his rabbit thumper dial goes to 11.

It would be handy dandy if a doghead had a off dial.

I would use that all the times.

Screaming Squirrels decided not to use the Anti-Weirdo Neighborling Fence. I know this because now I can hear hundreds of Screaming Squirrels on the roofer of my room. Hundreds running. Angus Doghead looks up and starts barking at the Screaming Squirrel feet you can't see. Then Squirming Squirrels jump off the end of the roofer onto the roofer of the Felix Porch of Viewing and then they jump on the garage roofer and then they jump onto the other fence of the backyard and yell, "TO THE BACKYARD THIS WAY NOW!"

Angus Doghead goes bananaboats and mom yells, "ANGUS! STOP!"

Dante Doghead goes loonyloons and mom yells, "HIPPO! STOP!" I still haven't told her Dante is not a hippo.

The squirrels jump off the backyard fence like a squirrel waterfall and yell, "TO THE OTHER SIDE!"

Mom lets Angus out because he is on her last nerve endings now. Dante is not allowed because he only gets his head stepped on by Angus and honestly you have to feel the sorrys for him because he is not a confused hounder. He is only a short stubby hippo-pittie that wants to sleep alot. Unless his roommate goes bananaboats. Then he feels the obligationings to go loonyloons.

I should talk to him about obligationings and how they are ridiculous. If you ask the Felix, obligationings are what gets half the confused going. The other half is thinking alone.

May 26th, 2020

As you know it was the memorial weekender. And let me tell you the whats, it was memoriabled around here!

First, dad got on the roofer and cut the Weirdo Neighborlings tree up that was banging on our roofer and not his. He had a ginormous buzzing saw on a stick. And he buzzed and the branches fell down. Right in the front of my Weirdo Neighborling Window. BOOM!

Weirdo Neighborling yelled, "Hey did that hit the roof!?"

Dad yelled, "I am not hearing you I have the earhole plugs in my earholes!"

Mom yelled, "Not your roof! Relax!"

Weirdo Neighborling yelled, "HEY! It sounded like a cannon."

Dad yelled, "I can't hear you!"

Mom yelled, "It didn't fall in your yard. Or your roof. It's not your problem."

Weirdo Neighborling yelled, "Well it sounded like it was the roof!"

Mom yelled, "Well it didn't. We aren't even near your yard. We're on our side of the fence!"

Dad yelled quieter, "Maybe if you took care of your #@*$."

Mom laughed.

I didn't know there was Weirdo Neighborling #@*$ over there. I am concerned.

Then the next day, dad power watered my side of the house and then the other sides of the house and all the windows.

That power waterer looks like a giant monster worm tongue sucking on my window. So awkward.

THEN because mom and dad were obviouslies energizing over the tops, they put new window blinders up on all the windows in my room. All of them. Dad had all the kinds of tools. And they all made ridiculous sounds. And then these new window blinders are the wrong color for my tastes. And alsotoo, nobody asked the Felix about this. They just did it. How annoying. How hard is it to walk over to the Felix and ask, "Hey Felix, can I ask you the questions?"

Felix says, "Why yes you can."

Mom and dad say, "We want to put up all new window blinders."

Felix says, "No."

The end.

Today I am going to throw everything out of the Felix Box o'Excitements onto the floor to watch mom chase dogheads to get all the Felix Box o'Excitements out of their drooly face mouths.

The end.

May 27th, 2020

Mom bought the new bed for Dante Doghead. His butt got bigger. And his head. His head is huge. Any theway. I laughed. Because everybody knows a doghead doesn't change beds. Trainers don't change digesting perches. Because we are not confused.

So, she brings in the new bed. Dante Doghead grabs it and jumps on it and murders it. I laughed. Out thelouds.

Mom took the bed and then actuallies took the times to explain things to a doghead. I so laughed out the louds.

Doghead sat in front of her wagging his butt rope and not listening. Mom believed he was listening.

"Dante, this is your new bed! It's orthopedic! It's soft and comfy and you will love it! Let's go upstairs and switch them."

Angus Doghead ran up the stairs and tripped mom who tripped Dante Doghead and the bed fell out of mom's hands onto Dante who murdered it. Angus ran down the stairs and stepped on mom's face and then helped Dante murder the new bed. Once mom said her kitchen was a hot mess.

The stairs were a hot messier. I laughed so hard out theloud.

Angus and the Dante dragged the still alive new bed down the hot messier stairs and murdered it right in front of me. Mom ran down the stairs and took the bed from them. Their butt ropes looked like helicopters. And they were drooling like komodo dragons. And panting. And sweaty. And honestly who would want a doghead now that we are talking about this hot mess?

Mom says, "Dante sit." Dante laid down.

Moms says, "Angus SIT!" Angus ran into the kitchen.

Mom looked at me and I said, "Do not look at the Felix. You never asked me about getting dogheads. I would have said, no."

She went up the stairs with the new Dante Doghead bed and Angus Doghead ran around the corners to run up the stairs and make them a hot messier again and Dante Doghead jumped up and ran up the stairs and mom ran faster up the stairs to beat them.

Hot.

Mess.

I couldn't see any thethings. But it didn't sound good.

Today the new bed is downstairs. Dante is napping on a different bed. Angus is digest napping on the floor mat in front of the hot messier stairs. And I am on my tree tent watching all the hot messed.

Of the course, if she had asked the Felix about the new bed she wouldn't feel like a hot mess right now.

But noooooooooo, no one asks the Felix.

May 29th, 2020

Just when I am thinking about nothing and relaxed something shows up. Dad says a guy is going to look at the sprinkling systems. Whatever that is that I don't care about.

So the guy shows up and knocks on the door. Which I do not care about. I am on my Felix Tent relaxing thinking about nothing.

Unthefortunetly Angus Doghead jumps and barks on the window at the guy that knocked on the door. Which shows you how confused dogheads are really.

The sprinkling guy knocked on the door and doghead barks at a window the sprinkler guy didn't knock on. Pfffft. Then Dante Doghead jumps on top of Angus Doghead and barks at nothing but Angus Doghead butt.

Mom looks at me and I look at her. I say, "You know where I am standing on all this doghead business."

She runs over and pulls Dante Doghead off Angus Doghead butt and looks out the windows sprinkling guy did not knock on and says, "Just a second."

I bet that sprinkling guy was thinking, there's more than one seconds of the confused in there lady.

Any theway, dad says, "Is that the sprinkling guy?"

Mom says, "It's the sprinkling guy!"

Dad says, "What?"

Dogheads are barking at each other's butts and mom is holding them by their doghead collars and she looks like she's on a carnival ride that isn't fun at all.

Mom says, "It's the sprinkling guy!"

Dad says, "I know! I am on my meetings hang on the second!"

I bet that mom was thinking, there's more than one seconds of this confused I'm hanging onto right here.

Any theway, dad goes out the garage door. Which the sprinkling guy DID NOT KNOCK ON!

Meanwhile, mom is still hanging onto the doghead collars attached to crazy butt barking dogheads that are alsotoo trying to bark at the window that the sprinkling guy did not knock on. And I can see him now in the window. He is looking at mom with the face I use when I'm looking at mom when she has one of those ideas that are not going to work for The Felix.

Then I hear dad say something I can't hear because the dogheads are still barking at each other's butts. Mom lets go of them and they fall down on the floor dog pile style. Mom says, "JEEZELOUISE and JELLYBEANS!" And then the dogheads run to the window where dad and sprinkling guy are talking about sprinkling systems I do not care about. And start barking at each other's doghead butts again.

Mom yells, "EVERY BODY is GOING IN A BOX!"

Dante Doghead is in a box. Angus Doghead is in a box. Dante Doghead is licking a cow toenail with the peanut butters. He sounds like he's snortle snorfling his butt. Angus Doghead is laying on his mattress of comforts panting like when after a good guy fights a bad guy and then the bad guy is beat. But now the good guy is a mess and he just stands there bending over and panting while another guy that didn't even fight the bad guy says something smart alecky.

I am not in a box because nobody puts the Felix in a box.

May 29th, 2020

Mom says it's a sunny shine day. I say yes it is! Alsotoo, I need a nap. Upstairs. In my Felix napping room roost cage.
Covered but not covered in the corner so I can keep the eye on the door alsotoo, the dogheads, who might sneak up and ruin my nap.

Alsotoo, also, the fan blows relaxationings into my nap if the corner is not covered.

It is quiet up here. I can move my bedroom towel into a circle to chew a corner of the circle nest I made. I chew and nap. It is impossibles to nap and chew. I tried that once and I don't remember if I got anything done.

Unthefortunetly I can hear lawnmowerings at the other Weirdo Neighborling's. And dogheads wrestlings. And Butters Dactyl yelling at turtles. I hear backup the trucks outside. What is going on already!? Obviouslies I am going to have to get the earhole plugs.

When I wake the ups, I am going straight down stairs and pooping on both dogheads' heads. That will show them who the boss is and what the boss is thinking about all that.

June 1st, 2020

The Foo Fighters sang a concert. They have the best beats for the feets. Mom says, "Hey! I'm going to learn a Foo Fighter song!"

I said, "No. Don't do that."

Mom says, "But I can do it! I'm going to learn EverLong."

I said, "No, it will take longer than that."

Dad went out the side to mow his grasses and mom said, "I'm going to sit here and learn the song, Felix. Dogheads are napping."

I said, "Don't blame the dogheads. That's my job."

So mom is learning the song and I am on my digesting perch. I tap my talons of beats for her. There's no points in telling her that she isn't David the Grohler, and the Foo Fighters would ask her to stop doing that if they were here. Eating breakfast or something.

Dad is mowing. Mom is learning she has longer than everlong, and the dogheads are snoring. Thankfulies she got the beats right, and she got the sounds right and if you don't expect it to sound like the Foo Fighters, or the David Grohlers then yes, she learned the song. I just tap my talons for her. It makes her smile. And get pistachios. Ever long.

Oh! Alsotoo, I watched a show called Barry. Mom said we were bingeing the Barry. I say you binge the pistachios and pretzel stickels, dip'n sauce, warm teas and those crunchy thingys I don't get enough. That's how all this works.

Any theway. Mom was very impressed with the show they binged and I watched. It was about confused fear of the losses.

The Hollywood has a hard time being originals. Which is confused. I really do not see the pointers for going over confused over and over with different actors. It's the same end. If it's a happy ending, they are still confused. If it's a sad ending, they are still confused. If it's the ending mom hates and throws popcorn at the TV, they are still confused. I think all movies should be named, "Let's Act Confused for Two Hours and then Stay Confused at the End"

So we finished Confused Barry and mom says the Cry'noutloud Virus will get in the way of more Barry. Personalies I think Barry got in the way of Barry.

We should watch more Foo Fighters.

June 2nd, 2020

Doghead bonked his head on the boat. Confused is inevitables. Now he has a head with some missing fur. Mom thinks he looks scalped. Dad thinks he looks good today and not scalped and his fur will grow back. Dante Doghead doesn't think. Angus Doghead doesn't care and mom keeps momming him with head washes and gooey gunk applicationings.

I saw the actioning. I hope the Weirdo Neighborlings didn't. How embarrassing. Chasing a squirrel and bonking your head and not catching the squirrel that stopped at the top of the fence to laugh at you and point a squirrely finger at your bonked head.

If anyone asks I am going to say he got into a fight with a badger that showed up out of the no where. The badger said he was going to badger him and Angus Doghead said, "No you won't!" And then they had the furious fights so big you couldn't even see it! When the dustings settled Angus Doghead was standing triumphantlies on the boat yelling, "TAKE THAT BADGER! AND DON'T COME BACK EITHERS! BECAUSE I WILL DOGHEAD YOUR FACE! AGAIN!!"

I told mom three times I didn't want to take the naps upstairs. When she tried asking number four I gave her the Eye of Exhaustion with the Eye of Disdains on top. I know it took her three months to stop calling me Franklin. I know it took one year to figure out her right is the other left which I don't like taxi service from. I know she is confused and thinks alone most of the times.

But a double dipper Eye Of to take a nap? That's why I have to take naps. Double Dipper Eyes Of are exhausting.

Which alsotoo, causes more problems any theway. Snickers Dactyl gets into my Box o'Excitements and throws things around looking for the things I haven't tossed on the floor yet. Hashbrown #annoying. I have to put every the thing back to take everything out again to toss the good stuff on the floor to get the dogheads in trouble to watch mom run in the circles after them saying, "Drop it." D r o p it!" That last part is hilarious.

I have to get all this confused straightened out around here. I have to get the busy campaigning for the Presidentialing. There's the big fishes to fry. Alsotoo, a small fish to beat. Cry'noutloud Virus Thingy or the not, the Felix Administrationing has the answers for the confused right now.

And they are not the Instarash Act.

There's already a virus thingy! We don't need insta rashes! Confused is so exhausting.

June 3rd, 2020

A duck pooped on the deck two times. Angus Doghead is running around the deck trying to find the duck. Cry me the rivers doghead. Now you know how I am feeling when you stick your licker tongue in my cage to steal Felix snacks I tossed on my floor for the later savor. I am going to write that duck the thank you lettering.

OMFee! Angus Doghead ate the duck poop. Next time he sticks that licker tongue inside my cage I'm going to climb to the top of my cage and drop my foods bowl on his head.

Mom is baby talking the baby ducks outside. Loud. I don't know if baby ducks don't have ear holes, or if baby ducks don't pay the attentionings or if baby ducks are actuallies baby deaf ducks. I bet mom is a Weirdo Neighborling to a Weirdo Neighborling by now, and she doesn't even know it.

She goes out with her yellow bowl and yells, "BELLO Little ONES!"

And then they run over and then the other ducks run over. And mom is throwing the leftovers parrots can't eat like yellow pellets. Cantaloupies cut wrong. Blueberries not the right round. The other half of the green beaner that wasn't the right half. The usual. She tries to talk in the french to the ducks. Out loud. Loud. "Venez ici petits! Je t'aime! Mes amours! Oh petits canards avec les petits visages que vous continuez à marcher l'un sur l'autre! Je t'aime mes amours."

If we have a Weirdo French Neighborling I don't know about, I don't even know to be embarrassed.

Butters Dactyl and I talked about this problem yesterday. You have to give a dactyl credit for talking about problems. Lurkers don't share their feelers like a dactyl.

"Mom is off her rockers, Butters Dactyl."

"HI!"

"We said hello already dactyl."

"HUH?"

"Dactyl, focus on the Felix. Mom is off her rockers and we have to stop her rocking."

"SNICKERDOODLE!"

"Don't call him over here! He is useless."

"Wanna drink ink?"

"No, dactyl. I want a plan to fix mom's rocker."

Unthefortunetly dactyl had no ideas about fixing mom's rocker. She just flew over to the couch and fell off the back of it. No the way was I going to ask Snickers Dactyl his opinion. He was hanging upside down from the giant tree stand licking a dangle toy squeaking like a doghead ball. He needs more help than mom.

It's lonely at the top.

June 4th, 2020

The rains are raining off and then on. Dogheads want to go out when it's on. Then in when it is off. Mom says words I'm not allowed to say and dad is looking for somebody to give him the break.

Dogheads are backwards. In is out, out is in, they eat the other thingy's poop for lunch, they dig the holes they don't use, they bark at nothings, they chase their butts and never catch them. I told mom and dad way in the beginnings. Remember if you think this is a good idea, it's not. Don't go backwards to go forwards.

But nobody listens to the Felix.

All the floors have doghead feet stamps.

Mom is running around with the eraser towel mumblings about something I warned her about. I don't have the time to tell her I told her so. I have the phonesbook to explode, and lunch.

There's the hurricanes again. I wonder if dogheads can get blown away in the CAT3. Or does it take the CAT4. Or does it really rain the cats and dogs and we just end up with more dogheads. And a cat that will probably leave once he gets in here and sees what is going on. Last hurricane it rained sideways. The dogs and cats probablies ended up somewhere else I wasn't.

Kirby Lurker said yesterday he heard Snickers Dactyl say to Butters Dactyl that mom said she wasn't going to stand for any of this ridiculous businesses any themore. Then she sat down. Never trust a dactyl to get anything straight.

Mom chopped my pears like apricots and my apricots like cantaloupes. My foods bowl is the hot mess. If I throw out the apricots I'll get more pears. Which I don't want. If I throw out the foods bowl Doghead is going to stick that licker tongue in my cage. She's left me no optionings but to act like I am the sick Felix. I'll sit in front of my crunchy stuff bowl and not eat anything.

Use the Eye of the Low Blood Sugars and wait.

But you have to be careful with all that because next the thing I know I will be wrapped up in a smelly burrito towel looking up the nose of Dr. NoseItAll trying to explain it's the misunderstanding.

My pears looked like apricots that looked like cantaloupes and the dogheads were in the house because it wasn't raining!

June 9th, 2020

Oh the boys, have I got the story for you. I will need three naps today.

Last the night after I told mom good night. And she told me good the night. And Snickers, and Butters, and Kirby, and the dogheads, she fell asleep. I stayed awake to make sure she stayed asleep. It's my job.

Snickers Dactyl woke up and decided to make his towel nest in the dark. His beak is noisy biting towels. I had to tell him to shush it and go back to sleeping.

Butters Dactyl woke up and decided to climb upside down inside the dark. Her clicky talons of ridiculous are noisy. I had to tell her to shush it, and go back to sleeping.

Kirby Lurker started buzzing like the radio talking to I don't even know who. His radio is noisy. I had to tell him to shush it, and go back to sleeping.

Then doghead borfered.

You know a doghead borfered because first, it sounds like a volcano of gerbils spitting out wads of wet wash raggers. Then mom yells, "Don't you eat that!"

Then I hear mom say, "Dante you borfered on your bed. What fresh hell is this?"

Dante didn't answer. He is a doghead.

Then I hear mom say, "Angus down, Dante down wait. WAIT. She whispers like she has a sore throat and yelling. Then I hear her say, "Out. Let's go out." And then the door opens and mom falls into the wall and the dogs run down the stairs and the door closes. Dogheads nail click and a door opens.
The problems with out is, they are outside my bedroom window, so they should have just stayed in any theway. I hear all mom's soar throat whisperings of the doghead desperation. She knows better to think they are actually listening to her.

Basically Angus Doghead wanted to chase a squirrel that wasn't there and Dante Doghead was walking in the circles without coming back to the mom who wasn't sleeping.

Then they come back up the stairs and back in the room and mom is soar throat whispering.

"Dante. Here."

"Angus, get in bed."

"NO, not Dante's bed, your bed."

"Dante here."

"NO wait, wait! I have your other bed, wait. No I. Dante sit. Angus sit."

They are not sitting or getting or waiting. They are wrestling.

Three times in the rows I hear all this happenings. Mom brings a new bed. I hear the bathing room door open and her dragging a borfered bed in there. Then mom ran out of beds. And I think her nerves. Because next the thing I know the sun is awake and dad is up and I am done making sure she stayed asleep even if she is not asleep wrestling borfering dogheads.

It's my job.

June 10th, 2020

Dad cut the grasses yesterday. Because it is growing a lot because it is raining a lot. So the grasses grow. A lot. He said cutting the grasses is not his favorite thing to do and he really doesn't like doing it.

I don't like looking at borfering dogheads. I feel his pains.

Dad says a sprinkling guy is coming over to fix the sprinklerings that spray water on the grasses so they grow.

Pardon the Felix, but maybe if you let the sprinklings stay broke and the water not spray the grasses will stop growing and you can not do the thing that isn't your favorite thing to do and then with all the extra times you can make the pancakes for Felix. Which I know is your favorite thing to do.

But I suppose no one will ask the Felix about this.

Mom and dad got a buzzing beeping collar to train the dogheads. Sometimes you think alone and then you have the hot mess alone. Angus Doghead hates everything now thinking everything is beeping. He is ridiculous running around trying to find the beeper.

Dante Doghead is wearing the beeper but doesn't even care it beeps. He cares it buzzes. Not a lot though. He cares enough to look around and say, "HUH, what was that I don't care about?" And then gets the doghead zoomies. Basicallies now the buzzer/beeper collar is a Zoomie remote controller. Mom's hot messes. Now she is being trained by dogheads.

Pardon the Felix, but that is my job.

Obviouslies this buzzerbeeper thingy is going to go into the drawer that has the other thingys in it that go into a drawer because you didn't ASK THE FELIX.

I will have to not drop things on Angus Doghead for the whiles. He's jumpy like the jumpy beans.

I met a jumpy bean once. He was in a box in a bean. Mom got him from someone who went somewhere. I saw the box and she opened it and in the box was a bean. Mom says, "Watch close Felix! There's a worm in the bean."

"Why am I watching a worm in a bean?"

She didn't answer. She just stared at the box with the bean with the worm in it and giggled like a gerbil. If you know a gerbil, you know what I mean.

I had to humor her and look at the boxed bean worm. It was a brown bean. The box was see the throughs and the brown bean was right in there in the middle. Mom stared at the brown boxed beaned worm. She looked at me, "The suspense is killing me, Felix." Then she looked at the brown boxed beaned worm. "I hope it lasts."

"The bean or the worm?"

She didn't answer. She stared at the box with the bean with the worm in it and gerbil giggled, again.

CLICK

I didn't see it. I just heard the bean bounce inside the plastic see the through box.

"FELIX!! Did you see? Did you see the jumping bean jump!"
"No. Is the bean dead now?"

She didn't answer. I looked at the boxed beaned worm because Mom's face was gerbiled. I can't look at that. CLICK click click clickclickclick

I saw the jumpy bean twitch inside the box.

"That's not a jump! That's a twitch. That's a twitching bean! What are we doing here?"

She didn't answer. She looked at the twitchy bean twitch, gerbil giggling and clapping her hands just like a hamster does.

I needed a beeper buzzer remote controller that day.

June 11th, 2020

I don't ask for the lots. I just ask for what the Felix should have. Mom forgot to give me seven pasta wheelies today. I tipped my foods bowl and it clunked and she ran over and said, "Don't dump your food Felix."

Dump my foods? A; if I was dumping the foods they would be in the sink now. B; I only have five pasta wheelies. Alsotoo; I only have five pasta wheelies. How can she possiblies get dumping foods bowl mixed up with missing pasta wheelies? I would spell it out for her but I don't have the pencil.

The sprinkler guy was fixing the sprinklers yester theday. He did not fix them yet. Dad was in and out and in and out of the door just like a doghead does. Talking to the sprinkler fixer that didn't fix his sprinklers.

Sprinkler guy left and dad said, "Well, something something something, and the something is broken and the sprinkler guy doesn't have the something part in his truck so he has to come back something sometime."

Dad could have just said, "He didn't fix it."

Mom said, "Well, I hope he can come back sooner than next month."

Dad said, "Yes, since now we don't have a working something sprinkler thingy. I don't know if we need a new something something, but he says it's the something. It could be, but I don't know."

Mom said, "Well, I guess we'll see something. Just get it fixed is what we want."

I was going to say something. But you know how I feel about having to say I told you so. Because I would have. If someone would ASK THE FELIX.

Mom tried to sneak in a new thingy in my foods bowl for the breakfasts. Not the pasta wheelie foods bowl. The other foods bowl. There's no room for sneaky thingys to eat in there. I would have told her that. She chopped up the mango. And put it next to my cantaloupies. Then the cantaloupies choppy squares fell over my apple chunks. I would have told her none of this idea chops was going to work.

Snickers Dactyl let mom bring him down the stairs for breakfast. He didn't even chomp her face. Or hand, or arm. I suppose the Spring is over now. Which is fine by the Felix. Spring brings Weirdo Neighborling outside doing the most weirdo thingys I see all the year.

Once Weirdo dug holes and put nothing in them. Who does that? Once after that, Weirdo walked around on his roof like a mountain climber I saw on the TV movie. But it wasn't snowing, or windy, and he wasn't running away from a wolf. Then after that once after, Weirdo had other weirdo friends show up and they all weirdoed together in the weirdo pool.

Floating weirdos all over a weirdo pool. Talking weirdo. Eating weirdo burgers.

It was CAT5 Weirdo Hurricane Seasonings.

June 15th, 2020

Butters Dactyl doesn't like it outside in the out side. Snickers Dactyl likes outside in the out side. Dad is powering wash dactyl cages, so they are in their outside RVs. Snickers is eating the nuts off the trees we have outside. Butters is hanging upside down yelling.

"THERE IS NO AIR CONDITIONING HERE!"
"I CAN'T BE OUT HERE! IT IS SO...OUTSIDE!"
"WHERE IS THE AIR CONDITIONING!"

Mom says she is a Devo. She is not. Devo is four guys wearing red round Lego hats pretending to be robots. They are hilarious. WhipIT! Whip it the real good!

Snickers just chomps on the nuts and looks at Butters like she is Devo. I guess I will have to explain that to Snickers later.

Dogheads are in cages. Dactyls are outside. And I have everything to the Felix. Which is pretty the nice. Mom is mopping the floors and telling me she loves mopping floors like she likes going to the dentist to pull her teeth. I didn't know she liked that.

I helped her with my bowls falling on the floor. Because I threw them there. To be super helpful.

The next thing I know I am in the Felix RV sitting on the deck with dactyls laughing at the Felix.

I'm pretty the sure mom was lying about mopping floors, or dentists. I will figure that out later.

"Welcome to the party. Butters is a mess." Why Snickers is welcoming the Felix I do not know. We already met before.

"SHUT UP! I can't stay out here in this THING. Where is my cage!? Where is my perch? WHERE IS MY DOOR THAT NEVER CLOSES THAT LETS ME LOOK OUTSIDE!" Butters is on the edge. Her eyeballs are googley water balloons and her face is wide open.

"Dactyl. Calm the down. You need to take the chill pillar." Hystericaled dactyls are cereal annoying.

"Feeman, don't bother. I've been trying to explain this since we got on the table. Hey! Do you have any peppers? I'll trade you my apple for peppers."

"I'm not trading anything! Your foods bowl is full of Dactyl Cooties by now." Snickers knows better. He knows he's covered in the Dactyl Cooties.

"I. AM GOING. TO DIE." Butters let go of the top, grabbed the side, and looked in the windows to see if mom was looking, and then let go of the side and rolled to the floor. And pretended to die. Which she didn't. She was looking around to see who was looking.

"Don't be a Devo!" Butters Dactyl was on Snicker Dactyl's last nerve ending.

By the time everything was put back together again and I was on my super cereal clean cage Butters was collapsing into her super cereal clean cage saying, "THERE HAS TO BE AN EASIER WAY!"

I think she should call mom's dentist.

June 22nd, 2020

Mom and dad took the five days off because their nerve endings were done. With nothing to do but take care of nerve endings you would be thinking, oh! Felix will get the pancakes!

Dad got the new pots and the pans for special cooking with the cast irons. And he got three new spatulas of the stainless steels. You will be thinking, oh! Felix got the pancakes!

Five days, Mom read books. Dad did the dad things but not the pancakes. Pots, pans, three new spatulas five days and no pancakes. Not one pancakes to test the new seasonings and the new spatulas. Does dad know his pots and the pans and spatulas could be faulted and not working at all? Obviouslies not. He can't know this until he makes the pancakes. For all he knows they are all broken and useless!

We need pancake testings immediatelies! But now he is working and mom is working and I am sitting here on my tree stand watching mom and not eating test pancakes.

This 2020 is getting on my last nerve endings.

Aunt Gini's Birdiebread Cones and Muffins mailed The Felix a box of the palm nuts to eat. I like the green ones, they fit my talons of fury. I do not know where she got the gigantor red radioactivated, mutant, weirdoling nuts, but if they hatch baby weirdolings, I will run out of nerve endings for the 2020.

The dactyls are eating them. If they become mutator monster weirdo dactyls I am opening the windows. They can go fly with the murder hornets.

Aunt Christine's Chop Shop sent a box of delicious talon tasty stuffings. Which one was a bag of new giant delicious fruits and the vegetables chunks. I like chunks. Her stuff is delicious every time I put it in my face. But then DOGHEAD stole the bag and ran off in the corner and Mom was busy with her nerve endings and DOGHEAD chewed up the bag that was for me. And chewed up all the good stuffs that was for me.

Mom found him in the corner with chunky treats for feets pieces all under his butt. I can't eat any of that.

June 29th, 2020

All the ducks are everywhere. All the ducks are alsotoo making the baby ducks. Mom has a duck friend who visits every day. Dad is outside walking the Angus Doghead waving his hands in the window to get mom's attention. Then he points to that duck. Then he waves his hands again.

Then doghead tries to snorfle a duckbutt.

Ducks have teeth on their tongue. He better stick to the snorfling of his own butt. That duck is on his last nerve endings with doghead butt snorfles.

Any theways, mom jumps up and says, bello little one!, and runs to the kitchen, out the dad garage and, there she is giving MY grapes to that duck. He does not shake his tail feathers as good as the Felix. She knows this. Then baby ducks show up and she gives them the Felix Grapes. Injustices!

If any more baby ducks show up there is the possibilities my pistachios will be pilfered. I will have to put Kirby Lurker on Pilfering Pistachios Alarms.

Yesterday Weirdo Neighborling chased mom's ducks with a broom. Mom said, "I'll chase him with a broom!"

I would really like to watch that happen. I bet mom would chase him so far away I would need another weirdo.

A woodpecker was woodpeckering on my house too early this morning. I need the Felix Beauty Sleep. He pecks really fast. And hard. And loud. He's going to get the head injuries if he keeps this up. And then he'll fall off the house. Mom will find him in the yard. Get a box. Put towels in the box. And water. And call him Jeremy.

She'll put Jeremy and his box in the bathroom closet to keep his warms. Then he'll woodpecker his box too early right behind my bedroom roost. And mom will say, "Poor Jeremy." And I will be forced to ask, "What about the Felix?"

And this is how I end up watching weirdos chase ducks with brooms. To take my brain off woodpeckering woodpeckers with head injuries.

July 7th, 2020

Today I watched the TVee Newsings. I won't do that again.

Last night at the bedtimes I let mom rub my head and my beak and I made the gooey baby bird sounds. This morning I told her no. You have to keep the trainings going and consistent. It is important to make routines and the schedules. Trainees just do better when they know what to expect. Trainees hate change.

Weirdo Neighborling is building a weirdo building in front of my face. He is using weirdo things to do it. Dad says he can't tell if he's building a wall or a mess. I say he's building annoying and I don't care what he thinks he is going to do with it in front of my face. Weirdo Doghead is helping him. Weirdo Neighborling says things like, "Give that back Dirty!" And then Dirty Doghead doesn't. Whatever weirdo is building in front of my face is going to take the times.

Alsotoo, Angus and Dante Doghead pee on the fence and on the Weirdo Building Parts when Weirdo isn't looking. The Dirty Doghead runs over and they all bark at each other and run back and forth and pee on the fence at each other. Angus Doghead spins and runs away back to the fence again. Dante grabs the fence with his face and growls. Once, Dirty Doghead peed on Dante's face when he did that. I laughed and laughed.

Mom says, "What's so funny Felix?" There's no point in explaining what I am seeing. I already told her she brought the wrong doghead home twice in the rows.

The firecracking was annoying again, even with four pancakes. Mom says, "GAH! It's like Beirut this year!" Dad said things I can't say and agreed with mom. Firecracking makes no sense any theway. It's confused with a fuse.

Then it rained.

Hard.

Angus Doghead is afraid of rain. Not lightening. Not fireworkings. Just rain. He hid up thestairs, then came down the stairs and walked in circles like elephants do with their heads down. Dante jumped on him from the couch and grabbed his leg with his face. Then they wrestled. Two wrong dogheads in a row. Because no one asked the Felix.

There's a green tree frog that lives under the porch outside. He croaks all the time because doghead's pool is out there and doghead splashes water on the tree frog. So he's happy all the time. Mom named him Jerry. I suppose I'll be dealing with Jerry and what he wants sooner than the laters.

July 9th, 2020
A FELIX PRESIDENTIALING CAMPAIGN SPEECH

Good the mornings! Hail! And Grey Strength to you! Today is like yesterday which is even more confused as the yesterday of the last year. That's right! Today I want to talk to you about The Confused. Sometimes confused is called politicals. Sometimes confused is called democraticals. Sometimes confused is called republicants. Sometimes confused is called "the news". It is all The Confused.

When The Confused gets mixed up in something like the Cry'noutloud Virus Thingy then that is confused. When the confused gets mixed up in the laws or the rules or even just the suggestionings, they get confused. You know where I am going here.

(Insert chants of CONFUSED HAS TO GO!)

I am running for the Presidential to eliminate The Confused where The Confused starts first. When I am elected I will immediatelies create the Universal Confused Care Act.

Once everybody gets confused care, this will help contain any confused that might crawl out of the corners and alsotoo, the crevices. Like worms. But not cute pink worms. Like the one that got in the garage last week and made mom scream and run into the house into a wall.

(Insert cheers for Universal Confused Care!)

I will immediatelies, alsotoo, begin The Confused Testings! If you caught The Confused it is best you shelter in your face for 72 days. If you have a Trainer, and you listen to your Trainer, you can come back out after three days.

(Insert cheers of WE WANNA KNOW WHO'S CONFUSED!)

We will also start the Contacting Tracings to know what is touching what. If broccolis are touching apple chunks no one has to eat that. I know I won't.

(Insert cheers of electionings that aren't confused!)

Goats4Votes will deliver two goats to every house that has a door and a smile when you open it! I have been talking to the National Brotherhood of the Goats Union and they are prepared to make sure all goats are Confused Free and ready to deliver the laughs to fight The Confused! Everybody knows The Confused has no funny bones. Laugh and confused disappears. Goats are on the front lines fighting the confused!

(Insert cheers of BRING OUT THE GOATS!)

These are weirdo times. Weirdo times call for extra Not Confused Actions! I will be the Presidential that grabs the confused and throws it on the floor! Like yellow pellets! Or the broccoli that touched my apple chunks!

Together we can fight the confused and once and for the alls be done with all of that ridiculous!

We all have the better things to do. I know I do. Yesterday Mom put a new Box O' Excitements in my cage. Without asking. I will have to throw all that on the floor three times!

(Insert whoops of hollers and Felix Signs waving in the air)

And so as you go out into The Confused and Cry'noutlouds Pantsdenim Virus Thingy, wear your masks! I'm super cereal. Wear Batman masks! So everyone knows you are super cereal! Alsotoo, no one wants to take the chances on getting confused in your nose or your mouth. That's grosser. Like Dactyl Cooties. Butters sat in my foods bowl and put her feet in my food the other day. Dactyl Cooties were everywhere. I didn't look at that until mom said, "What's the matter Felix? Don't you like lunch?"

"NO!" I said with the authorities! "NO I don't like lunch with Dactyl Cootie Sprinkles! Do not be confused about that!"

(Insert WE HATE COOTIE SPRINKLES!)

Do not be confused! Vote Felix! Vote Parrot Party! My Vice Presidential Angus Doghead asks for your vote today, for NO CONFUSED TOMORROW! You may be thinking, but The Felix, why a doghead inside the Parrot Party Tickets? Because! Dogheads are very good at sit, stay and roll over! Vice Presidentialing is pretty the much just only that anyway. I am not going to waste a perfectly good Trainer on the Vice Presidentialing.

(Insert chants ROLL OVER ROLL OVER! SIT AND STAY! CONFUSED CONFUSED GO AWAY!)

Show your supports for the Parrot Party and The Felix Campaign by wearing a tracking device and sharing the hope and the dreams of NO MORE CONFUSED! Together you can watch me take care of the businesses!

(Insert screams of TAKE CARE OF THE BUSINESSES!)

Thank you for my Supports! And remember only YOU can choose NOT CONFUSED!

July 16th, 2020

OH the nos! The Felix House has a leaker in the roofer. Or maybe the leaker in the pipes. I don't know. I know a plumber guy showed up and walked around with dad to look at the thingys and talk about waters. That guy kept talking to the Felix. "Well hello Felix, do you talk?"

Do I talk? Nobody has time for this! There's a leaker in the roofer or the pipes! Get the busy. The Felix is not a circus act.

So then the plumber goes upstairs and dad is downstairs. Then dad goes upstairs with buckets of the waters and the plumber guy stays down the stairs yelling up the stairs, "Okay! Pour it!"

Then dad comes down the stairs and they talk about stacks, and pipes, and roofers, and waters, and leakers. I am busy helping mom chop the cantaloupies. I have to test pieces in the case they are poisoned. I am also keeping the eye on this guy. He is wearing the masks and the gloves and booties on his feets. I saw that in a movie once. That guy folded up dead guys in carpets and then threw them in a van.

Nobody is folding my Mom and Dad up in a carpet!

Any theway. Plumber guy and dad are in the kitchen talking to mom and mom is chopping the cantaloupies and I am testing for the poisons. The guy says, "Felix, you sure are good lookin!"

Yes. I am. What about the leaker?

Then he says to Mom. "Does he talk?" (Just for the records any thebody asking that question about a Trainer needs a Trainer immediatelies.)

Mom says, "Yes, yes he does."

"He's pretty quiet." Says the plumber not talking about the Leaker in the Felix House.

Mom says, "You are irrelevant to him. If he was a human child you wouldn't get a conversation, either. You don't belong here. You don't belong to his flock."

This is why sometimes I'm pretty sure I can train her. Alsotoo, I FeLOLed.

"Oh! Well, I want a cockatoo."

Mom says, "No you don't." And then mom trained him. I watched and ate the not poisoned cantaloupies.

Then the guy says, "How old is your water heater?"

Dad stopped listening.

Mom says, "Older than this leak. Let's talk about the leak."

It cost $59 dollars to get the plumber out of the House of Felix.

And now dad says, "Well it's not plumbing; it has to be the roof."

Then it rained. And then dad said, "It's the roof."

I'm pretty sure it's going to get really weirdo around here.

July 17th, 2020

Two guys showed up yesterday to do the inspections of the plannings and to handle the businesses of leaks.

Dad says he doesn't have time for this. Mom says she doesn't have the smarts for this. Felix says I don't have the nerve endings for this! Let's get somebody the else to do it!

One guy talked to mom. One guy talked to dad. Then both guys and dad talked about the leakers. And then they took pictures. Of the leaker, not me. Who does this?

Dad said, "Ya! There it is!" And just like that, the leaker wasn't in the roofer and it wasn't in the pipes and it wasn't annoying as much as it was before. Then dad and the guy made the plans, and the other guy talked to mom about the plans and I was right there and he didn't say hello. I was right there on my tree stand thingy right there with mom.

He says, "Did you paint all these murals?"

Mom says, "Yes I did."

He says, "Are you going to finish that wall over there. This is great!"

Mom says, "I painted all these before we brought home parrots. I can't see how ladders work with them now."

She laughed. He laughed. He did not say hello to the Felix. I was right there. She said parrots. That's me. He didn't say hi.

The other guy didn't say hi. Then they left behind giant humming whatever machines in Snickers' bath time sink room. You see where this is going.

I looked at Snickers. "This is weirdo."

He looked at me. "I'm going to bite them all."

Then another guy comes in the house and says hellos and he is the Hvacuumer guy. And I am right there! On my tree stand thingy testing broccoli for the poisons of death. The Hvacuumer guy says, "Wow!"

And then I get ready to say hello.

And he says, "Are those lizards?" And points to Rotini and Donetilli lizards. BEHIND ME IN THEIR GLASS BOX HOUSE which I am in front of! He didn't say hello to me.

Mom says, "Yup. Those are leopard geckos."
"Wow. You've got a lot of animals. This is cool."

I then get ready to agree that I am cool.

And then he says, "Hi there buddy." Which is the improvements even though my name is not buddy.

I say, "Here." Because he has a pen I want immediatelies. And I hold out my talon of fury to take it from this Hvacuumer guy.

He laughs. Mom laughs. No one gives Felix the pen.

Then he talks to dad. And dad and this guy tear apart the walls again. And talk. And tear apart the walls. And I keep testing broccoli, because no one will give me that pen I want immediatelies. Then he said he would go back to his Hvacuumer office to get the parts and come back today.

He better bring that pen.

Today is mom's birthday. She didn't ask for birthday pancakes. Who does that?

Supposedlies somebody is coming back to the Hvacuumer workings. I don't know. Dad called them and the girl that answered the phone was so confused mom looked like a genius to me. Mom says, "WHAT!? Did she just say she doesn't know anything?"

The girl says, "I won't let you fall through the cracks."

Mom says, "We're already under the sidewalk!"

Dad says, "Calm down, it's your birthday. Relax."

Mom says she has the Birthday Rages.

AND THAT is because she did not ask the FELIX about the BIRTHDAY PANCAKES.

July 20th, 2020

The Hvacuumer guy is coming over today.

He better bring that pen.

Mom says she is now a Mealworm Farmer.

I watched her farming. I saw those wormers. Just when I am thinking I have all this under the controls, she decides to farm the worms. She feeds the lizards a worm with a pincher thingy. And then she stirs up her worm farmer box and says, "Ooo, look at all my worms. Felix! I'm farming!"

No, you're not. You're annoying.

I asked the lizards about this problem. Rotini said she didn't particularly much care a lot. Because to her way of the thinking, worms are worms no matter what farmer got them. Donetilli said he didn't care because he has better things to think about. Which I am not believing. They live in a glass box. I can see all the things to think about in there.

Mom was on the phone talking to the State Farmer. I thought they were talking about meal wormers, but then mom said, "We already paid the plumber and the Hvacuumer guy."

Now I know she's confused because she paid that guy and I didn't get that pen.

Today I have to test the poisons in cantaloupies, broccoli and mom says she is going to chop other thingys. I will have a lot on my plate. I also have to get that pen. I will get that pen.

The mower guys are outside mowing the grasses outside our yard. They ride mowers super fast like race cars but without all the drinking and shouting and flags, and circle. They just go fast in all the directions.

Mom says she will throw things at them if they harrassel her ducks. Dad doesn't say anything to that. I would like to see her throw things at the mower guys to see if she can do it. I throw things at the dogheads, it isn't as easy it looks.

Dante Doghead had his ears washed out yesterday because mom says he has hippo ears that catch everything. All I know is when he shakes his hippo doghead head his ears sound like the helicopters. Angus Doghead doesn't have the hippo ears. He has the hound ears and I guess they don't catch everything or any the thing. But now Angus Doghead is harrasseling Dante Doghead to snorfle his earholes. Mom says they smell like lavenders now.

I have a lavender hippo doghead that sounds like a helicopter.

No one asked the Felix if I wanted any of that.

But I want that guy's pen. I will get that guy's pen.

July 22nd, 2020

Guess the what? I got that guy's pen.

Now I am going to throw it on the floor one hundred million thousand times. And make mom pick it up one hundred million nine hundreds and ninety nines times.

July 23rd, 2020

Now that I have the Presidentialing Pen of Word Making I will be writing the speeches of not confused.

This is a good pen. He forced me to take it. By leaving it on the table.

Any theway, Weirdo Neighborling forgot his pants.

Cry'noutloud Virus Thingy is still here.

Mom is sheltering in my face.

The Hurricane named Gonzalo is heading to the Felix. Nobody has the times or nerve endings around here for the Hurricane. Florida is on its last nerve endings, mom said so.

Tree Frogger is making all the frog rackets because it's raining hard. Maybe he is breeping his Hurricane Alarm. He could be. Butters Dactyl has a turtle alarm when the turtles show up to walk around. Tree Frogger will come in the handy if he is a Hurricane Alarm Systems.

Doghead tried to lick him yesterday. Tree Frogger was on the window and frogging to himself and then Angus Doghead ran up to him and stared at him. Mom said, "Leave it."

Angus said, "Why?"

Mom said, "Angus, you leave Jerry alone. He's busy doing his thing."

Angus said, "Yes, I want that thing."

Mom said, "Angus, Jerry is not ..."

Angus Doghead licked him. Jerry's eyeballs popped out of his head in his face, "HEY! Don't snorfle my frogger butt doghead!"

Mom shook her head like she does when Dante Doghead slides off the couch on his head, on the purpose.

Mom is definetlies on her last nerve ending.

The constructioning guys are supposed to come today and look at the wall that is gone that the leaker was hiding behind. If they ask the Felix, they should leave that wall gone. Mom just runs into them anyway. One less wall is a good thing.

But nobody will ask the Felix. And mom will just run into the new wall. Then I will have to shake my head like I do when she runs into the walls thinking alone.

July 28th, 2020

The leaker is fixed. But the fix broke the thingy not broke. A new Hvacuumer guy came over and ignored me. He didn't even see the Felix. Or try to see the Felix. Or give me his pen. I'm pretty sure he has a pen like the other guy. He looked at the things and said, "Oh ya, it's all wrong. I will fix that wrong for you no problems."

Dad says, "Well, that's great!" He didn't tell the guy to give me the pen. He could have. He was right there. They were shaking the hands. He could have said, "Hey, guy, while you are at its, give The Felix your pen. He wants it."

But no one asks The Felix.

The campaign is picking up the speeders! Tracking devices are linking up to the Felix Satellites. I see where everybody thinks they are going. I have a lot of the work to do.

Weirdo Neighborling came out theside yesterday with no shirt on. He had the pants. Which saved me from the awkwards. But no shirts. Weirdos are wiggly.

They should keep all that covered up, if you ask the Felix.

There are baby ducks all over outside again. Mom gets cereal exciteables about them. She runs out the front door with her yellow bowl of whatever baby ducks eat. She runs out the back door with her yellow bowl of whatever baby ducks eat. She runs out the garage door with her yellow bowl of whatever baby ducks eat.

I am keeping the eye on my Pistachio Stash Jar of Deliciousness.

"Bello!" she yells. "Bello, mes petits amours. Viens! Venez ici! Le petit déjeuner est prêt. Mes petits amours. Tony! Ne marche pas sur la tête de Jerry!"

She likes talking like minions and french duck ladies. Tony and Jerry are boy ducks that show up and annoy her. I feel her annoyings. Every the time dogheads show up and annoy me.

Dante Doghead is hunting giant bugs that make mom scream. The Hvacuumer guy and the other guys took walls away and they are still not put back. Good point; she can't run into a wall that isn't there. Bad point; the bugs that make mom scream are running around from the outside from the open walls. I guess. What do I know about Palmetto buggers. Except they make mom scream.

GAH!!! Then Dante Doghead shows up and snorfles bug butt to death. I saw it with my own two eyeballs. He stepped on that bug, and snorfled it's butt. And then it was just a mashed up snorfled to death brown leggy thingy. After he killed it, his buttrope wagged really hard and banged my Tree Stand. How rude. Butt Snorfle somewhere else doghead.

Then mom gets paper towels, and covers her eyes and picks up the butt snorfled bug. And she screams really quiet. Like a balloon squeaking out air.

Dante doghead ran over and knocked her down. And she almost fell on the dead butt snorfled bug body. I thought she died of the heart attacks. It's not even time for after breakfast before lunch snack attacks and this place is razzle dazzling.

July 29th, 2020

Dad has the meetings on his laptopper. He says the important things. Then somebody in the laptopper says important things. They must be super small and skinny to fit in there. Butters Dactyl yells every the time dad says the important things.

Dad says, "Butters! Please!"

Butters says, "RAWWWWK!"

Dad says, "Butters!" And then says to the little skinny people in his laptopper, "Sorry guys, Butters just can't not talk when I am." Little skinny people laugh.

Obviouslies dad doesn't understand the Butters is saying important things, alsotoo. I would tell him that, but nobody is asking the Felix. Butters thinks if she flies all over the places it will help dad understand. Personalies I understand blowing all dad's papers and thingys around won't help much. Except the doghead who wants to steal them. But nobody is asking the Felix.

There is the hurricaner in the Atlantic heading to the Felix. Somebody should just shut the Atlantic Door. I would, if somebody asked the Felix. I bet Jerry frogger will like all that hurricaner rains. I saw him on the window last nights chasing a bug. Not the bug that makes mom scream, a different bug. Mom said rats and snakes eat the Palmetto Buggers. I did not need to know any of that.

Mom has a lot of the TMIFFs. Too much information for The Felix. I have to use the Eye of I am Pretending To Hear you But I am Not Listening. I tried the Eye of Not Listening, once. She didn't even care. So now I use the Eye of Pretending. At least I can think about breakfast in the peaces and she thinks I'm thinking about the TMIFF. Which I am not. I do not need to know about how she is going to put traps for the Palmetto Buggers. But then she has to touch them later. And what if Doghead tries to snorfle the Palmetto Buggers when they are in the trap? And what if she has to touch them later after that?

Touch what? The snorfled bug? The trap? The trapped snorlfed bug? The doghead? What is going on!?! The problems with the TMIFF is there are no factuals in them. Lots of the panic and the fears and the loathings. Which I do not have the time for any theway.

You can't fix confused if you listen to TMIFFs. I would tell her that, if she would ask the Felix. But no one is asking the Felix.

July 31st, 2020

I am energizing! Last nights the dogheads didn't wrestle at all and I got the beauty sleeps. Mom looks like she needs more beauty sleeps. She says she feels like she slept with drooling weasels last night.

I do not want to know any more than that.

Yesterday dad trimmered the tree.

This morning mom brought in the trimmered branches and stuck them all over the dactyl cages. Now there are dactyl cage bushes in here. When they fly down here they are going to shredhead all that. Then the floor will be all sticks. Then the dogheads will grab sticks and chew sticks and throw sticks and slide sticks and drool sticks.

And then mom will blame every thebody else on the mess. So. Confused.

There were no mom screamer bugs yesterday. Dante Doghead tried hard to find one. He moved the couch. The chair. The other chair. The doghead bowls. The Horde cage. The other Horde cage. My tree tent. The dactyl giant tree on the wheels. And all the towels on the floor to catch poop from dactyls that always miss. Why she puts towels down for them is unknowns. They don't aim for them.

Any theway. Dante moved everything. Mom moved everything back. No mom screamer bugs. I hope there are some today. So hilarious!

Hurricaner Isaias is coming, but now it's not coming to The Felix side of the Florida. Just the rains. Isaias only has one cat. No big dealer. I hate them when they have five cats. Mom gets the hystericals. She gets the 5 cat hurricaner stuff. And always forgets the emergency pistachios! Most the likelies when there is a hurricaner with five cats I will die of the low blood sugars and not the hurricaner.

Mom read me some of the Kurt Vonnegut book. She says, "You know Felix, you are the Kurt Vonnegut of Parrots."

I'm pretty sure He is the Felix of Trainees.

Mom finally made new Felix Campaign Presidentialing Propaganda Tracking Devices! There is a Christmas Tree ornamentals with the Santa and Felix on it. Because Santa endorses The Felix. The other guys are on his naughty list.

There is a big puzzle of the Felix with the Angus. It is 500 pieces. The perfect puzzler for the parrot party propaganda campaigning! It's like putting a exploded phonesbook back together again. Only not so exploded.

There is mini collectible buttons for mini collecting. In the case you don't have a lot of the space.

Campaign fun raisers are excitables, alsotoo. Mom made the matching shirts to go with the Felix Mask of Don't be Confused. Because only weirdos don't wear shirts ...or pants. Of the course fun raisers are for Trainers in the needs of things. I don't need anything except. VOTES!

Dante doghead found his butt rope this mornings. I don't think he knew it was his all this time. I think he thought some other doghead's butt rope was following him around.

Now he chases it so fast he gets pretzeled and the crazy eyeballs. Like a doghead butt rope chasing hurricaner with no cats. Just crazy eyeballs.

August 5th, 2020

Mom rushed my Pasta Wheelie Enjoyments Before Breakfast Snack. The Hvacuumer guys are coming early to make more mistakes I guess.

I can't just "eat Pasta Wheelies" on my cage top. Firsts, that's not how this works. Seconds, I can't.

This much confused this early is inappropriations and rude! She even hasn't had her coffee fuels, yet. Those Hvacuumer guys are in for it. They don't even know!

One time dogheads were running around the house and mom didn't have her coffee fuels yet, and they almost knocked her down, stole her pillows, barked, stole her blanket and slid on it, into the front door like boulders. Mom yelled, "EVERY BODY in a BOX!"

I bet those Hvacuumer guys end up in the dogheads' boxes. They don't even know.

August 6th, 2020

The Hvacuumer guys fixed the fix. And did not talk to the Felix. Or have pens. The whole thingy was the disappointments. Two Hvacuumer guys and not one pen.

Mom didn't yell, "EVERY BODY IN THE BOX!" one time. She didn't get on her last nerve ending at all. Dogheads took naps. It was so boring I took the naps. And then when I woke up when one Hvacuumer guy said, "Goodbye, Felix."

That is fine and dandruffs, but where's your pen, guy?

I am excited to see all the Felix Masks already ready to go. Can you imagine the confused looking at the Felix face on the Constituent face?

They will be, "OH! I AM confused! It is the enlightenments." And then they will go home to their house of confused and tell them, "HEY! We are confused. Let's stop that."

I am energizered! Monday the August 19th, I will announce the TAG TEAM CONTEST for constituents. The rulers are simple. Because simple is not confused.

The top 10 most taggers on the Felix the post will receive the full set of the Felix Campaign Button Tracking Devices. And the top tagger will receive all those and a beakographed and signed Felix Direction for the Confused book, alsotoo.

I'm pretty the sure the excitables will be generated! It is time to share the Not Confused!

I got the idea watching the wrestling matches on the TV. There was four wrestlers tag teaming and wrestling. VERY exhilerationings! BAM! and then the tired wrestler got out of the wrestling ringer, and the not tired one got in. Then I thought, "HEY! I get exhausted, too. It is time for The Felix to TAG TEAM!"

Monday will be cereal.

If the Hvacuumer tag teamered the pens, thingys would have been different. But, nobody asks the Felix.

August 10th, 2020

You know those other guys are confused when they mess up the mailsman so bad I can't do my TAG TEAM CONTEST. Just one more reasonings to put The Felix in the Grey House. I will have to poster pones the contest until this whole "make the mails go super slow and alsotoo, don't mails packages at the same time as the envelopes." Who does that!? Cheater cheaters, yellow pellet eaters, that's who.

Mom called the mailsman and asked is this for reals. She has the connections in the places. Because of The Felix. I have many trainee mails peoples. Which is why when I am elected the Presidentialing, I will fix this in the one minutes.

Any theyway. They said in the Florida it going to get hairy for the sure. And most liklies mails to other places will be hair ballers. Which gets hairered in the world.

"Hairy like a doghead?" I had to know specifically what I am dealing with.

"No, Felix. Not a doghead." (She could have said that first.)

"Hairy like a cat?"

"No, Felix."

"Hairy like that coat you have you say is fake hair? That thingy is ridiculous."

"No, Felix, not like my faux fur coat."

"Hairy like the sasquatch!?"

Mom thought the minutes and said, "All in all that pretty much explains everybody and everything confused, Felix. Yes. Sasquatch Hairy."

Sasquatch Hairy Confused. I didn't even know I had to fix that! It's whatevers. I will fix The Sasquatch Hairy Confused at the same time as The Confused.

Mom is messing up my naps. She rolled my roost cover backwards not forwards and so the fan blew my peek the boo corner around like a flag. That is Sasquatch Hairy Confused for the sure.

Every time I fell asleep my peek the boo corner blew into my cage and poked my nosehole. Then I'm awake again. This is not a nap. This is ridiculous in the dark.

Mom took the Dante Doghead to Doctor NoseItAll to get weighed and to get his flea's medicine. I didn't know Doghead's fleas were sick.

Mom said Dante is Fifty one and the halves pounds of hippo. I hate to be breaking the news but he is fifty one and the halves pounds of Sasquatch Hairy Confused. Alsotoo, he is not a hippo. Dad says they should have called him Tank. I could have told them to call him, "NO, we don't want that one. He is a Hairy Sasquatch of Confused." But. No one asked The Felix.

When I am Presidentialing I look forward to everyone asking The Felix. Yes to Not Confused. No to The Confused. Double No to the Sasquatch Hairy Confused. Top secret meetings in the ovaling offices will be super cereal short.

Then I will come out for the Pressing Conferences and announce, "We are eliminating the Confused!"

Then I will take the Presidentialing trip to the Congresses of the Senegal Senate and the House of the Representing

Cockatiel and Conure and I will say, "HEY! Eliminate the Confused. Have the nice days!"

I will Cheeto the confused bills. (Which of the course, there won't be any confused bills, Because Trainer.)

Any theway, this Cry'noutloud Virus Thingy plus the Cheater cheaters yellow pellet eaters is getting on my last nerve endings. I am not going to look out the Weirdo Neighborling window today. I can't the even.

August 13th, 2020

Today mom stopped crying. I'm not going to ask her to train for a while. I will give her the Eye of Love, and the Eye of Adorationing, and the Eye of the You Can Scritch My Head. She is going to need all that for the whiles. Not crying is not feeling the better. Not yet.

Kirby Lurker was a great Vice Presidentialing runner mate in 2016. He was cereal successful as a Blanket Worm Hunter, Lurker, Yellow Pellet Pitcher, and alsotoo, hilarious. He told me a joke once.

"Knock knock."

"Who's there?"

"I threw all your yellow pellets on the floor!"

We laughed and laughed.

Mom says she doesn't have anyone to chew holes in her shirts. I suppose I could make this a hobby. Mom says she doesn't have anyone to surprise her by landing on her shoulder. I can't do that, flying isn't my thing. But I will make her Taxi me more. Keep her mind off the things that aren't there.

My yellow pellet ratio is going to be higher now. Who's going to throw out the ridiculous from my foods bowl in the morning? I can't touch any of that. I have the no idea how I am going to handle keeping the eye of mom now without the Kirby. He was my Mom is Thinking Alone Warning System. I only have two eyeballs.

I have to find a new Director of the Feather Bureau of Investigationings for The Felix Administration. Blanket Worms are at the all time high. I have to find a Lurker with a Blanket Worm track record immediatlies. Ironicallies, The Confused and Blanket Worms go hand in the annoying hand.

So here I am, and there mom is trying not to be what she really is right now. Super Cereal Sad. I appreciate her trying. I know why she is doing it. But you can't fool The Felix. You can fool a dactyl, but not The Felix.

I suppose I will let her scritch my head. Fluffer my fluffers. Nuzzle my noser. And rub my Talons of Fury. For now. I will throw all my toys out of my cage more, too keep her busy. I will alsotoo, most the likelies, let her kiss me more. And if she is still not alright, I will go ahead and take the nap with her on the couch. I'm not going to say all this outlouds to her. She will get clingy and sticky. I suppose she can be needy right now.

I'll let her be needy. She needs that right now.

When I am elected Presidential I am going to rename the Washington Monument, the Kirby Lurker Pointy Tall Thingy and paint it blue. And make the Medal of Lurker signifying excellence in Blanket Worm and Confused fighting.

In the honor of the Kirby I will find a Lurker Sanctuary to donate all the proceeds of the Because Parrot Fun Raiser. In the name of all the Lurkers still working the hard Training and fighting Blanket Worms.

But today I am needed for the comforting of the mom. Probablies tomorrow, too. She's a mess. More of a mess than her normal hot mess of confused.

August 17th, 2020

I discharged mom from her needy snuggling prescriptionings last night. Treating the sad so it doesn't get confused is tricky businessing. I let her kiss my beak, rub my talons of fury, scruffle my fluffles, floofer my fluffers and pet my head for three nights. I administered the Eye of Adorables and the Eye of Agreeables AND the Eye of Snuggle Festing.

This is cereal Trainer Medicines and you have to know when to stop other the wise she gets addicted. Nobody needs that. Particularlies me.

"I know what you did Felix. You didn't have to stop though. I wasn't going to get all clingon or annoying." She chopped my cantaloupies in the squares. "I really love petting your head and floofers you know."

"Yes, I know these thingys. HEY! That's a triangle. Be careful with my breakfast."

"I'm just saying, you know, I have more time on my hands now and more room for, you know, more scritches." She chopped my apples into rectangles. "I really love petting your head and fluffles you know."

"Yes, I know these thingys. HEY! That's a square! Be careful with my breakfast. You brain is wondering around again. Alsotoo, I know how much your hands have more times for confused. I see that square apple."

"Well, maybe tonight you can change your mind about scritches." She laid down her chopper. "I won't try to scritch you during the day. I know that's wrong. I won't try to scritch you on your tent. I know that's wrong. I won't even try to sneak a scritch. I can control myself."

"No, you can't. You put the chopper down and breakfast isn't done."

Then she put eight Pasta Wheelies in. EIGHT. I'm supposed to get 11. Eight, she's is discombobulated. This is the sure sign of The Felix Withdrawals. I cut her off just in the times.

I am now obligatored. The last thingy Kirby said to be before he Lurkered away was, "Take care of her."

"I will." I said, "I will."

Now that I am thinking about 'I will', I think that leaves a lot of the rooms for interpretationings. I will wait for eleven Pasta Wheelies for the sure.

August 21st, 2020

Mom said 2020 should take the hikes and then used words The Felix can't use. There is another hurricaner coming toward The Felix! It only has one cat. Which is good. I have two dogheads. I'm pretty the sure it will have no cats after it leaves.

Yesterday Angus Doghead went to Dr. NoseItAll to get the check up on all his doghead parts. Mom got the home and oh the boy, did she have the story! She came in the door asking all the questions right off the batter.

"Angus! What is your deal?"

Angus Doghead was rolling around and hopping like a rabbit that can't hop right.

Dad stopped the typing and said, "What's wrong? What happened?"

"Well you know it's not good when you're handed doggie downers without asking for them. He lost his mind in there I guess, and helicoptered poop and pee and vomit everywhere."

"Is he okay?" Dad was concerning.

Mom looked down at Angus Doghead snortle snorfling his butt. Alsotoo, panting and smile drooling.

"Oh sure, he's just fine. Just stellar."

First, I want to know where Angus found a helicopter to ride at Dr. NoseItAll. I never saw one when I was there. Secondlies, is everywhere where I go when I go to Doctor NoseItAll's. Because if it is, I am not going in there ever again.

Today mom said good the mornings to a gazillion baby ducks in the back of the yard of The Felix. Then she giggled and squealed like a leaky balloons and ran out the door with her yellow bowl of duck treats. WHICH better not have any of The Felix treats.

Without a Lurker, now I have to do all this treat inspections myself. I better write that down on the Felix To Doing Thingy List with That Guy's Pen.

Mom went shopping to the stores yesterday and alsotoo, campaigning while she did that. She was Twofering! She gave out the Felix Campaign Tracking Devices and told every thebody about Goats4Votes, No More Confused, and the Universal Confused Care Actioning.

She said she talked to a lady that was undecided (confused) about who to vote for, and after talking to her about her undecisioning (confused), the lady said, "Well if I had known about a Felix I would have stopped listening to those other guys a long time ago!" And then she put on her tracking device, which is working great. She's getting the coffees at Starbucks right now.

Mom gave out 23 million tracking devices yesterday, or something like that. The Felix Campaign of No More Confused is rocking and rollering!

August 24th, 2020

What is the problems with taking Pasta Wheelies to bed for a snack attack nap? Nothing. Unless you are confused and you are mom and you think you have the better ideas. Which she doesn't.

Here I am in my nap, with nothing in my face to crunch. I'm pretty the sure a nap and a crunch can go together.

The fanner feels pretty the nice though. The dark is just right, I can see everything through my peek the boo opening. Except a Pasta Wheelie. Which if it was still in my face would make this just right.

Next time I am hiding that Pasta Wheelie under my floofers.

Now that I am relaxationings it is obvious morning napper needs to be morning napper with the snack attack backer. It just makes the sense.

Mom sits on the couch and snacks. She laid on the couch and snacked once, alsotoo. Now that I am really thinking about all this, obviouslies she knows just how much a snack and a nap go together!

I'm hiding two Pasta Wheelies under my floofers next time.

Yesterday dad made the sunny sides up eggs and the tater chunks and bacon bits. I told mom I wanted to eat at the table Felix Style. Alsotoo, Weirdo Neighborling was in my window weirdoing in the overdrives. I can't eat and see all that overdrivings. I ate the breakfasts with mom and dad and mom put extra sunnies and chunkies and bits in my foods bowl for later snacks. Sunday is snack attack day.

SaturDADday was uneventfuling. Dad played the Batman XBoxer to beat the Joker. Mom read another book. All. Day. Dogheads did the naps and mom said she wasn't going to walk a dog because it was 107 degrees outside. That's the first sensibled thing she has thought alone.

It's so hot out, Felix Popsicles turn into Felix Puddles.

It's so hot out, Felix Outside Deck of Viewings and Breezes turns into Felix Sauna of Death.

It's so hot out, Weirdo Neighboring's weirdo melted.

No it didn't. That's just wishfulling thinking. His weirdo got sweaty. So much sweaty weirdo.

The hurricaners are not coming here. They are going to Louisanas. I'm pretty sure Louisanas does not want any of that. Even if they only have one cat each, that's two cats. And one big hot mess.

Mom says Hurricane Seasonings is a rodeo. I don't know about all that. I do know that when there are more than no cats things get cereal weirdo around here. I don't have time for any of that.

I wonder if I can fit a cantaloupie in my wing pit next time?

August 25th, 2020

Mom ran out of the baby duck food. She said the Barbarians were at the gate and she could not a peas them. Well, one pea isn't going to fix anything any theway. She said she has to go out and get more foods for the ducks.

What about the Felix? My Jar of Pistachio Savings Accounts and Snack Attack Safety Backups is at 43 percenters!
But no. No one asks the Felix how close to death he is today of the low blood sugars. I am 43 percenters away of no more Felix! That's how close.

Ducks will eat any thing. Any Thing. I saw one eat a lizard! That duck chased that lizard around my Deck of Viewings and Relaxationing Breezes and caught him by the head and swallowed it like a sketti noodler! Who does that!?! I saw a duck eat bugs flying around the grass. I saw a bunch of ducks doing it. As if this is the normaling thing to do. Eating flying bugs. They eat it all. They don't even ask the questions of the thing they are swallowing!

I bet they eat yellow pellets.

Any theway, you can see how confused mom is when she is cutting up the grapes and the blueberries in tiny bits for the ducks. That duck swallowed a lizard! I'm pretty the sure you could feed him a square apple and he'd swallow it.

Next week is the Parrot National Conventionings. We have the things to do! And here she is worrying about ducks that swallow lizards whole and thinking, "Oh the NO! My ducks will die of the low blood sugars!" There are lizards all over the place.

All the baby ducks walk right through the chain linker fence to come in the yard and barbarian around. The mom duck flies over it. Then they look around distracting my mom who I am training. Then she has to get her lock key to unlock the fence to carry the yellow bowl outside the fence and feed the ducks who run through the fence to get to her and that yellow duck bowl of food that should be AFTER The Felix gets fed. Then she walks back in, locks the gate and then the baby ducks spill back into the yard like little teeny peas through the colander that annoys mom when she is trying to clean the teeny peas.

Dante Doghead had to pee so mom had to take him out on his doghead Lasso of Controls. Which the control part doesn't work much. And he was there and the baby ducks were there. And he snorfled a baby duck butt! Then mom duck ran up and hissed at him saying, "STOP SNORFLING MY BABY!"

"Who are you?"

"I am the duck that will teach you a lesson!"

"Good luck. You see that person at the end of this "leash" attached to this "collar" around my neck?"

"Yes."

"She thinks it controls me."

"Well, she sounds confused."

"Ya, we've agreed to that in the house."

"Just stop with the snorfling my babies. It's inappropriate, awkward and unnecessary."

"Fine. You're not that interesting anyway. I'm going to over there and pee on that rock."

And after he peed on the rock, mom brought him back in the house to snorfle Angus Doghead's butt who wanted to go outside and chase a squirrel up a tree. Which mom did not let him. Because the baby ducks laid down for the after breakfast before lunch nap.

I suppose the Parrot National Convention will all be my work. These ducks have mom looking at the wrong things at the wrong times.

I'm exciteables about the PNC next week! We have the speakers of epicness! First BATMAN will be speaking and endorsing the Felix. He said he has been working on the speech between fighting the criminaling activities.

Then Santa Claus said he will be, but he has to Zoom in because the reindeer are asleep. But it will be stimulating. He said those other guys are all on his Naughty List again. They didn't even make it to September.

Then Werthers, President of the Brotherhood of Railroad Engineers and Piggles, will give a speech. Very impressive.

Then Angus will give the speech of the Vice Presidentialing Candidate. I read his speech. It's not confused.

Then I will give the big time candidate speech.

There will be the exciting Upload a Video of Supports! event. And there will be TAG TEAM Constituent Event.

So much to do, so many tracking devices to get up the linked. Mom is in the backyard in her pajamas talking in French to sleepy baby ducks. She has no priorities.

August, 26th 2020

Mom and dad said no more Hvaccumers or the plumbers or the other guys are coming over any themore. Mom and dad said, they paid them what they wanted and now they will do the rest of the whatever is left, themselves. Something about the State Farmer and a deductibler and alsotoo, somebody is dragging their butt too much.

I guess they have a doghead.

Any theway, that means no more pens to get. BUT I have the excitable news! I decided like a Greyt Presidentialer that I will fix The Confused. The Confused being no more guys with pens.

I got the Presidentialing Campaign Pens with the helps of Aunt Christine! A good Presidentialer always has good connections that are not confused. The Parrot National Convention next weeker will be so excitables! Pens to win! Pens to buy! Pens to get! And there is a NEW Felix Campaign Trail Mix flavor! It's super cereal. I can't even tell you right now Diary Thingy, it's so super high cereal secret.

I'm pretty the excited about the pens. Mom and dad said they don't need those other guys and their butts dragging. I, The Felix, do not need their pens either, alsotoo!

And I don't understand what the other guy's doghead would be helping with any theway. Angus and Dante Dogheads drag their butts in the house. In the yard. On the porch. On the couch. On each other's head. And nothing gets better or gets fixed. I think mom has the unreasonable expectations. Which is the symptom of The Confused.

Today Dante said hello to mom's baby ducks. Mom said the barbarians stormed the gates and then went out with her yellow bowl and Dante Doghead. She can't do that with Angus Doghead. Angus Doghead thinks ducks should be herded into duck puddles. Then he ruffs and hops like a gazelle, and then he stares at mom. The ducks are not impressed.

Dante said hello to the mom duck. She was not impressed. But one of her big babies walked right up to Dante Doghead and said, "PEEP!" Dante jumped backwards.

"WHAT are you doing?"

"Saying hello."

"Why?"

"Why not?"

"What are you?"

"I'm a Durden."

"A Durden?"

"Yes, Durden Duck."

"You smell funny."

Then Dante snorlfed Durden's buttfeathers. Which wasn't the good idea because then mom duck got involved.

"HEY! Get your nose off my baby YOU WEIRDO!"

And then all the baby ducks ran over and puddled between the mom duck and Dante Doghead and they started yelling! I couldn't believe my eyeballers!

"WEIRDO WEIRDO WEIRDO! YOU GOTTA GO! WEIRDO WEIRDO WEIRDO! MOM SAID SO!"

Then mom duck walked through her baby puddle and said, "YOU dog, are in over your head."

Dante sneezed and ran to mom, who was standing behind him, laughing and grinning.

Sometimes you gotta be wondering what is going on in the head of a trainee mom.

OH!!! More exciteable newsings about the Parrot National Convention! I almost forgot.

Wonder Woman will be speaking and endorsing the Felix! AND Darth Vader will be speaking and endorsing the Felix! That's right! Vader decided to leave the Dark Side, and come the Felix Side. The Felix is strong in the Force. Nobody knows this, but I was Yoda's Trainer. I don't like to say that much because then, it sounds like I am braggalicious and name droppering.

Any theway...

The Parrot National Convention is going to be super excitables and stimulatings! Contests! Avengers! Vaders! BATMAN! Contests! Winnings! Tracking Devices! Pens!!! Oh.

I think I popped a buttfeather with all my excitables.

August 27th, 2020

Dante Doghead decided to sleep with mom last night. I know this because I heard this.

-Whiny beggy, whiny beggy doghead noises-

"What's up, Dante?"

-Whiny beggy, whiny beggy doghead paw scratches on the mattress that mom doesn't want him doing-

"Do you want up here? Okay hang on."

-mom falling on the floor-

"Ouch. Oh boy, Dante it's dark in here, huh?"

At this point I am having no hopes here. Because it is nights. She turned off the lights. She knows these things.

-mom grunting and umphing helping a hippo on a bed sounds which sounds like two hippos if you ask The Felix-

Dante doesn't help mom get up on the things. He just asks. I watched mom help Dante onto the couch once. She got his front on, then lifted his back. Then his front fell off. Then she put his front up and his back fell off. Then she said, "Dante don't be a slinky!"

At this point I am having no hopes. He is not a hippo. He is not a slinky. But no one asks The Felix.

Any theway, she is in the darks pushing a slinky up the side of a bed and not getting both ends to stay the puts at the same time. I can hear all of it.

"Dante help me here, bud."

He's not going to help her. But no one is asking The Felix.

"Dante. Just. Get. _rumpgh_ Up. There. No not that leg first. Wait. Dante use your."

-mom falling on the floor-

Then Dante makes the snortling snorfling sounds. I do not know which butt is getting all that, and I am glad it is dark. Then it sounds like a hundred dogs are running in circles. Then it sounds like mom is on her last nerve endings. And then I hear a doghead on a bed scratching the blankets and snorfling a blanket nest like I do. They do blanket nests on the couch. With the Felix Blanket. Which I am still waiting for mom to ask me about because I have the opinion about THAT.

Any theway, then it is dark. And quiet.

Except for Dante snoring. He sounds like a bear snoring. I know this because I watched a show about bears hibernatering and they snore. They sound like a Dante Doghead. But they didn't say that in the show. Mom said it was educational animal informations. But they didn't even say bears snore like Dante Doghead.

I watched Neil DeGrasse Tyson talk about planets one time. He didn't even talk about Planet Felix. There's a Planet Felix out there. NASA named it. They made it the big deals. And Neil Degrasse Tyson the Astrophizzysist didn't even say anything about it. Oh sure, he talked about Mars. And the Uranus. Which I suppose a doghead would be interested in snorfling.

But, no one asked The Felix and Planet Felix.

August, 28th, 2020

Doghead did not sleep with mom last the nights. I know because I heard her snoring. Not like a bear. Not like a doghead. Like a mom who didn't have to push a slinky.

Mom went essentialing yesterday to get the essential snack attack tastes. She did not get the essential pistachios. My Pistachio Jar of Savings Accounts Snacks and Backups is at 37%. THIRTY SEVENS PERCENTAGINGS! Obviouslies mom essential is not The Felix essential and I need my own debiter card and Zon Primer to get the missing 63% pistachios.

If you are wondering; Do parrots do math? Yes. Yes we do all the maths. Walnuts. Almonds. Pistachios. ALL the maths.

Weirdo Neighborling was hosing his porch off and chasing ducks off it to hose it. Mom giggled and covered her mouth looking out the window.

"Oh Felix, I'm pretty sure he doesn't like our ducks. I probably drive him crazy feeding them."

First, what a Weirdo likes is always confused. Secondlies, being Weirdo, he already drove there.

Mom and The Felix watched him spray and hoser his porch and then he hosered a duck's butt. Mom said, "Oh, H E helicopter! NO!" She ran out the door with her yellow bowl.

Then she started feeding the ducks a second breakfast! Weirdo went into his house. Then mom shouted BELLO! and started talking French Duck Lady. "Est-ce que ça va penelope? Votre cul est-il mouillé? Comme cet homme est impoli! Je suis dégoûté! Ici, prenez un petit déjeuner plus délicieux et ne vous inquiétez pas pour lui. Quel bizarre!"

I am not a French Felix so I have no ideas what she was saying, but all the duck butts were wagging so it wasn't confused, I guess.

Any theway, a baby lizard came into the house and mom said she had to save him without hurting him to get him outside to be safe from dogheads. There's mom, crawling around on the floor, talking to a baby lizard. Dogheads are in their boxes to keep the lizard safe. They want to help. A lot.

"Here little lizard, let me help you."

She crawls around and the lizard runs under a dactyl cage. Mom looks at me like I have anything to say about this, I do not.

"Felix, why do they always run under the cages?"

"I don't know. Why do you always keep my Pistachio Jar at danger levels?"

"Come here little lizard, you do not want to meet Angus or Dante."

Which is ironical. I tried to warn her about all that way in the beginnings when mom and dad said, "We need to rescue a doghead." No. No you don't. I would have said. But, nobody asked The Felix.

Then she crawled around the Felix cage because the lizard ran under the towel on the floor that I make sure to miss every time.

"AH! Gotcha!"

Mom stood up and there in her hand was a teeny tiny little long lizard. He looked straight into my eyeballs.

"HEY! Get this woman off me!"

"Sorry lizard. You should be feeling lucky, you could be wrapped in a burrito towel."

"A WHAT!?"
Mom smiled and talked right to the lizard's face.

"Aw, little lizard, you're safe. Let's go outside and find a good bit of safe monkey grass to live in."

"I just CAME FROM THERE LADY! What are you? A Weirdo!?"

Mom walked to the front door and I yelled to the lizard, "She's not a Weirdo, that's the guy with the hoser next door!"

August 31st, 2020

Felix felt it important to hold the Parrot National Convention the week immediately following the other guys' confused conventions. To prove The Confused they own.

The following are transcripts from the PNC speakers and their endorsement comments.

Mom opened the Convention. Felix insists we warn you to take everything she says with the grains of salts. Unless, it's about Felix.

WELCOME to the 2020 Parrot National Convention here in sunny St Petersburg, FL!

As The Confused Mom I open this year's convention and proudly admit my confusion and Felix's skill to assess these things.

Our speakers this year are impressive. I'm excited to open the floor to their words and thoughts. As we look at the future I take note as to how similar we all are as citizens.

The Right are like Captain America, wanting justice and strength.

The Left are like Ironman, confident wanting to create gadgets and ideas that fix all the problems for good.

The Progressives, call to mind Spiderman. Friendly, caring, working hard to make all the neighborhoods safe.

The Independents, by their name, much like our beloved BATMAN. Ready to jump in, wanting to jump in, and defend right against wrong. Ready to work alongside those willing to work as hard. A bat signal shining from the tallest building.

As a country we are Star Wars. 330 million story lines based on a family issue that goes way back. Those issues, although 330 million versions, have the same core. The Confused.

Confused begins where communication ends. And then we forget where we thought we were going!

FELIX, Felix knows where we think we are going. Every day he stops me and reminds me of my own, misdirection. I run into far less walls thanks to The Felix. I know with love and gratitude, that Felix wants us ALL to run into far less walls.

Felix has been training and teaching others for 8 years now. Watching him humbly present the dangers of walls and The Confused has been an inspiration. Children call his name. Adults pause in their confused thoughts and breath sighs of relief. There is something about this bird, that inspires every one that meets him, to smile. Confused hates that.

The Confused fears The Felix because confused requires us to fear, judge, and eat round cantaloupes. Confused requires us to forget our way, stop laughing, stop listening, stop lounging, and stop loving. Oh, The Confused is real.

The Felix is real, too. He doesn't want power. He doesn't want fame, legacy, or money. He just wants peace. And quiet. And no confused. And no yellow pellets.

Felix is here to bring Goats for laughs and joy. Universal Confused Care so every one can find the care they need. He has the plans. He has a Cockatiel and Conure Congress ready to step up and into the problems of the current horde. He has a Senegal Senate prepared to replace the current congealed and cognitively challenged barbarians at the trough.

He has plans to liberate all the colors of the pellets, so all can choose their own snack attack paths!

He has the plan to use the power of the Land Managements to plant tens of thousands of trees. Walnut, Pistachio and Pecan.

He will kick out the drillers, and frackers, and clackers, and confused land suckers. He will return the natural beauty lost to those that can only take.

He will remind us all that we are one big messy, loud, raucous, short, tall, fat, skinny, quiet, reading, singing, eating, sleeping, pooping, bathing, climbing, sliding, throwing, calling, whispering, feathered, skinned, furry, scaled and soon to be NOT CONFUSED family! We are all on the same planet racing in a circle around a sun in space. We are like NASCAR, but nobody wears their sponsor's logos.

Felix will fix that, too! There is no swamp. There is only The Confused.

And now, I give the floor to our first Speaker.

A man we all know. A man that has served his Gotham City and knows about family issues and how they become The Confused! I give you The BATMAN!

DAY 1
Featured Speaker – The BATMAN

Hey.
It's me.

BATMAN.

Welcome to the 2020 Parrot National Convention!

You're probably thinking, "Hey, BATMAN. What are you doing here?"

That's what Felix first said to me when we met fighting crime. You know. Crime is a symptom of The Confused.

I was apprehending a criminal, as per usual BATMAN. Felix was in Gotham, staying at the Waldorf Astoria. He wasn't put off by my dragging a criminal by the Bat Rope, down Park Avenue. I liked him for that. Nothing throws this bird off. He's so knee deep in fighting The Confused. He's focused. Like me. The BATMAN.

I told him I was dragging this pile of trussed up crime to the GCPD. Felix nodded. We talked about his arch nemesis, Toothbrush Holder. I told him about mine. The Joker. How both our nemesis continued to escape. We realized that night that we had kindred crime fighting spirits.

In this year of The Confused, it's harder than ever to see the truth. Felix cuts through the chatter, buzz, fat words, fluff talk, bantered wasteland of verbs, and constipated conflagration of confused conversations, to the core of all our communal concerns. The Confused.

I am proud to endorse Felix R. LaFollett for President of the United States. I'm hopeful. Not so dark. With Felix at the helm of our great country, we've all got a partner in fighting confused in the highest office of our lands. The People's Office.

The People's White House. The People's ...

"PSSSSSSSSSSSST..."

The People's Gr ...

"PSSSSSSSSSSTTTT! batman...pssssssssst....pssssst!!"
"What is it, Felix? I'm endorsing you."
"It's just that...get to the pistachios..."
"OH! Oh ...yes. Pistachios ...almost there Felix."
"OH. Okay ...greyt ...I'm just excitables is the alls."

The People's GREY HOUSE!

Felix has proven time and again that the only thing to fear is fear itself! And High Yellow Pellet Ratio. Alsotoo, Low Blood Sugars ...

"FELIX. I didn't write this ...did you put this in my speech?"
"Maybe."

Felix is the No Confused Candidate. And by that very stature he inherits the Law and Order candidacy, the Strong Economy candidacy and the Joining Together candidacy. Now I'm more of a stand alone kind of guy. There are a lot of stand alone kinds of us. Felix supports OUR rights to be left alone while joining together! Which is not confused at all.

As a child of Gotham, this country, and this world I am confident Felix will lead us all to No Confused. After that, everything should pretty much be o k a y ....

"FELIX! I didn't write that end. You changed my ending."
"Mine's better. Keep going! You sound the greyts!"

I look forward to supporting Felix after he wins The White House and changes the name to The Grey House. I look forward to fighting the confused and all it's criminal elements. As a Crime Fighter, I will proudly move forward as a Confused Fighter!

Felix, the Batarang, BATmobile, Batclimber, Batcrawler and BATcave are ready to work along side your administration!!

"PSSSSST!!! Can I ride the BATmobile?"
"No. There's only one seatbelt."

Felix felt it important to slip in a few parrot viewpoints after The BATMAN. The floor manager lost a buttfeather having to move scheduled celebrations around.

The Felix keeps you on your talons.

Hail and Grey Strength!

Thank you mom, for not being as confused as I expected!

Thank you BATMAN, for being The BATMAN. Alsotoo, you should have Alfred make the technology upgrade to the BATmobile and get another seatbelts in there. When I am elected Presidentialing, I want the BATmobile to be the Presidential Cool Taxi. That would be super cereal cool. And you don't even have to call it the FELIXmobile.

You could, though.

(Insert cheers and the gasps for the FELIXmobile!)

I am looking forward to this week extravaganzeled, exciteables, and actions! Parrot Party is where The Confused ends.

I am inviting all my contituents, supporters, and Felix Followers of Epic Attentionings, and Appreciations to make a Video, or write a post in the supports of the Felix here, on the Felix Page, all the weeks long.

The Confused really hates it when we work together. The Confused can't even handle all that cooperationings.

(Insert shouts of the NO MORE CONFUSED!)

Post a video! Post a speech of your own! Post pictures of your propaganda! Post pictures of you! Post pictures of your Trainers! All in the supports of Felix and Angus and The Parrot Party! The top 10 Support Posts will win The Felix Campaign Button Tracking Device Collection AND The Presidentialing Pen! It doesn't matter if you video or just post. I am not judging on fancy. I am not judging at all. That would be rude. Let's have the funs! Let's celebrate being together! Confused really hates it when we do that.

(Insert the cheers of FREE STUFF!! TRACK ME TRACK ME!!)

This is the first of opportunities to win and be tracked. This week is over the tops of wowzer!

Additionalies you can find your own tracking devices and Propaganda goodnesses at my The Felix Propaganda Store here: https://www.cafepress.com/imwithfelix

AND you can get all the Felix Campaign Trail Mixes and Flavors for Snack Attacking here:
https://christineschopshop.com/felixs-snack-attack-emporium

And remembers! All your Propaganda and Snack Attack shopping goes to help parrots in the need, sanctuary, and rescues. Alsotoo, do not worry, I have Elon the Musk shooting satellites up into space to support all the tracking devices you can fit on you.

(Insert cheers of SPACEX! ELON the MUSK! Science!)

I know where you think you are going!

Alsotoo, thank you for my delicious and nutritious surprise box of pistachios from my Canadian Guardian Pistachio Angel! My Pistachio Jar of Savings Accounts and Snack Attack Back Ups is at 100%! Until lunch.

You are super cereal appreciatinged! I will not have to worry about the Low Blood Sugars all Convention Week!

I alsotoo, told mom she could share some with the dactyls and crush some up for the Horde. Because this week is super exciteables and sharing is caring! Until dinner.

And so I invite you all to make your words, voices, and faces and post your speechers all week! Join me, The Fee, win propaganda and tracking devices! The Confused really, super really, cereally hates it when we laugh, work together, and support each other.

Grey Strength!
Vote Felix!
Bring Pistachios! #Felix2020

September 1st, 2020

Just because it was Convention week, doesn't mean the weirdo wasn't happening at home.

This morning Dante Doghead borfered on the floor again when it was dark, and mom fell out of the bed. I don't know if mom falling out of a bed made Dante borfered, or Dante borfering made mom fall out of bed. OR if mom fell out of the bed because she does that.

I do know I was asleeper and then I woke up to mom saying, "ouch!" And Dante Doghead saying, "GACK!" No one needs this ridiculous in the dark.

Then mom says, "Don't eat that, Dante!"

You have to say these instructions to dogheads. Dogheads do not read their own instructioning manuals.

"Don't eat that."

"Don't pee on the floor."

"Don't poop on the floor."

"Did you eat this pillow?" (The answer is always, yes. Why she bothers asking after the first pillow is beyond the Felix.)

"Don't ride The Felix's Tent Stand like a skateboard!"

"Get out of the garbage."

"Get out of the piggle food."

"Get out of the bunny food."

"Leave it."

"Drop it!"

"In the box!"

"Down!"

"Not on Dante's head!"

"Not on Angus's head!"

You will probablies be thinking, 'Hey Felix, did your mom read the doghead instructioning manual?' I would be saying, "Obviouslies not. She adopted them anyway."

Any theway!

The Parrot National Conventioning is on the fires!

Constituents are posting up and participating! I am cereal exciteables! I will be busy reading all the participation posts and looking at the participation writings and videos and alsotoo, super supporting shouts of successes!

Werthers Macintosh, President of the Brotherhood of Locomotive Engineers and Piggles will be speaking today. He is a very great wheeker speaker! I am emotionaling just thinking about what he will say.

I am feeling The Felix Fire!

Day 2 Parrot National Convention
Speaker – Werthers Macintosh

Welcome to Day Two of the Parrot National Convention!

I am not a parrot.

The obvious needs stating loudly as of late. I assume that it's best to keep that trend going! I stand opposed to confused!

I stand united with Felix R. LaFollett!

I am Werthers G. Macintosh. President of the Brotherhood of Locomotive Engineers and Piggles. I am a Wisconsin born, Floridian transplanted piggle. I have been a member of the piggle brotherhood my entire life taking the reins of leadership through union voted support and handed down from my father, Harold L. Macintosh. My father was a progressive piggle, and union supporter.

My father faced heavy burdens when he first arrived in Wisconsin. Forced to change the family last name from Mencken to Macintosh, thanks to some guy writing absurd opinions about absurd people.

My father, of strong stock, would not abide his family being cast into that same lot as absurdity. Hence having found himself in a field of trees dropping delicious Macintosh apples, he took up the name. My father taught me tenacity in the face of absurdity. Felix showed me absurdity is but The Confused. That all things itchy, twitchy, and tasteless begin in The Confused.

I met Felix at a Piggle Condo Association Meeting. He flew in out of curiosity and stayed for lunch. We spoke of many things that day. Snap peas, green beans, apples, oranges, and other weighty matters. I found him serious, focused, and not easily distracted.

The type of bird that will look The Confused in the eye and say, "NOT ON MY WATCH!"

We're on the ground, we piggles. We face The Confused head on everyday. The Confused is found in the small things in as much as the large things up there.

We see the confused for what it really is! Food delivery delays. Ask yourself, do you want confused at all, large or small? No! I say! NO!

Ask yourself, does confused help anyone in anyway? No! I say! NO!

Ask yourself, do I harbor confused in my heart and pantry? If you say yes, my hope for you is illumination of that confused. Illumination that leads to eradication that delivers emancipation! NO. MORE. CONFUSED!!

Felix knows where we think we are going! He is ready to stand tall, stop our fall, and walk us to our destination of NO CONFUSED!

Felix has proved himself worthy of this trust. Felix gave us the book, *Directions for the Confused*. He knew then as he knows now, the only way out is through THE CONFUSED!

And through we shall go. We shall mount up and mount a campaign! We shall walk. We shall crawl. We shall slither, dither, and stalk! We shall lurk, we shall fly, we shall swing, fling, and dive!

We shall meet this moment in the time of The Confused. We shall not wither nor wain. We shall not pause, or fain. We shall face that thing that needs no name. And together, we shall beat The Confused!

And after that, everything is pretty much okay!

The Brotherhood supports The Felix. And I, Werthers G. Macintosh, endorse him with full piggle power.

Join me! Join the movement to end The Confused.
I thank you for your voices! I thank you for your time! I thank whoever is getting lunch!

Day 3 Parrot National Convention
Speaker – Santa Claus

Initially Santa was scheduled to ZOOM into the speaking engagement. With the Cryn'Outloud Virus Thingy it seemed the best choice.

Last minute Mrs. Claus put Santa on his sleigh and said, "Get out there! This is too important to sit in Santa's Chair and talk! Rally the bird and his continuants! Be the Santa I love!"

(This quote comes from an autonomous elf source with access to the Claus Mansion)

HO HO HO!!!

Merrrry Parrot National Convention! Welcome to the third day of a rousing convention event!

The last convention I went to wasn't half this fun, and it was the National Christmas Elves Convention, sponsored by Bud Light.

hohoho ...I see so many on my good list here today. And a few on my naughty list. Hooho ...I'm looking at you Gary.

HOHOHOHO!

As Santa Claus it is my job to identify nice and naughty. As Santa Claus it's also my job to overlook the lists, merge them, and hand out hope wrapped in bows.

That's how I see Felix today. Hope, wrapped in grey feathers. Delivering the Eye of Discernment to all matters at hand. He knows it all boils down to The Confused. Doesn't matter what is going on. Felix is the cookies and milk after a long day's work.

I met Felix years ago after he wrote me a letter warning me of The Confused wrapped inside a neighbor. After some investigation by my elves, I found he was right. Made some adjustments and safely delivered Christmas cheer. I wrote him back, and we became great friends through long distance letter writing.

I appreciate his humor and fearless approach to The Confused. For Felix, The Confused is just the thing that needs staring at long enough. Sooner or later it will give up. But you have to see it. And that's where the Felix Administration comes in!

In 2016, I endorsed Felix for President. Four years later I still stand behind this parrot. I stand behind his running mate. Angus Lee is a good boy. I gave him a bone last Christmas. He'll get another one this year. He's a constant on my good list.

I stand behind the Parrot Party and it's principles of fairness. Loud calls of joy. Treats. Gifts. Tossing confetti made of things created by joy. I believe in the Parrot Party because the Parrot Party looks up! They fly high, not low. The Parrot Party reminds me of my tiny reindeer. Small packages, with great big hearts.

I bring word from Mrs. Claus today as well. She stayed behind to make sure the elves tend to business. Last time we left together for a vacation things didn't go as planned. We found elves in the hot tub, the reindeer drinking all the root beer, two windows were broken when they tried to jump off the roof into the pool. Christmas trees were in the pool instead. It was a hot mess on a cold night.

Mrs. Claus is an amazing wife. She puts up with more than most. And she sees through The Confused with almost as much skill as The Felix. Almost. And so let me read to you, her thoughts for this great day.

"Hello from the North Pole!

As the wife of the most famous and generous guy around, you know me. When Santa told me he'd be at the convention I felt I needed to add just a few words about our beloved Felix. He saved my husband from a Weirdo Trap. I hold him in high regard. He sent me potpourri with a lovely note that read; 'Dear Mrs. Santa the Claus, this is not a bribe. I hope you like the smell. It is pistachios and cinnamon. P theS, can you make sure Santa read my letter I sent. Thank you! Felix LaFollett'

The best part of Felix is, he is Felix without one additional word of obfuscation. He is who he is and you get what you see, which is a magnificent Felix. Ready to serve, train, and nap. Well, you just can't ask for more than that now, can you? I will vote for Felix.

Mrs. Santa Claus"

You can see my wife has strong feelings about our Candidate. As do I. I'll leave the podium with one final thought. When choosing someone to look over you, lead you, inspire you, and fight The Confused. Never choose from the Naughty List.

The House of Claus endorses Felix R. LaFollett! Because those other guys are on my naughty list every single year. Thank you! *HOHOHOHO! Let's GO!*

Day 4 Parrot National Convention
Speaker – Wonder Woman

Day 4 of the convention proved magical. Two speakers approached the campaign manager offering support through endorsements and speaking directly to the constituent base.

Felix was over the couch with joy.

Welcome to the 2020 Parrot National Convention! Parrot Party is where The Confused ends.

I am, Wonder Woman, and I am proud to endorse Felix R. LaFollett for President of the United States.

The Felix Administration will be TOUGH on confused. It is long past time to put a Grey in the White House.

You have heard from Batman, my fellow Justice League member, that Felix is the Not Confused Candidate. Grey Strength will toss The Confused right out the White House door.

This is, of course, as important to the League as pasta wheelies and pistachios are to Felix! Our crime fighting against criminals can only be as strong as our battle against The Confused.

Let us move forward into no more confused by putting Trainers in the Senate and the House of Representatives! Today with the Felix Campaign, we can know where we think we are going!

With my Lasso of Truth I pledge to help Felix rope the symptoms of confused!

The Felix Administration's Double Goat Anti-Confused Project is directly aimed at The Confused. Take Two Goats and laugh! Confused doesn't like laughing and goats are hilarious so there will be less confused with Felix as President.

I also pledge my personal super hero work; *http://www.thegalacticalliance.com/about-us/charity/* and all it's powers to creating laughs, and joy to fight The Confused! The Galactic Alliance is available to all who seek such remedy as super hero hellos! Visit out website of revelation to learn more about our work, and how we will support the Felix Administration!

I am Wonder Woman, and I endorse Felix for President!

And now it is my honor to introduce to you a man who has seen the Dark Side of The Confused. Has fought his way out, and into The Felix Side!

DARTH VADER!

When Darth Vader walked to the podium, Felix lost a buttfeather.

I am Darth Vader. Dark Lord of the Sith. I am Luke's father. I am no longer confused, and I am proud to endorse Felix R. LaFollett for the President of the United States and the Galaxy, if he so chooses!

This is not about World Domination. This is about The Confused. The Confused seeks the world to dominate. The Felix seeks only that which is fair, righteous, and honest. And tasty. And not yellow.

I met Felix while investigating a disturbance in The Force. I intended to turn him to the Dark Side. I was blinded by the Dark Side. But Felix with his Talons of Fury and no nonsense suggestions, turned me to the Felix Side! The Felix is STRONG in the Force.

I was confused. I know this now. And I now know he can fix the universal confused. Grey Strength will create the Universal Confused Care Act, under which everybody is entitled to confused care, and pre-existing confused will always be covered.

The Dark Side doesn't care about yellow pellet ratios or pistachios because The Dark Side IS The Confused. The Confused must be eliminated where The Confused has taken deep root! Those other guys!

Felix and his administration of towering Trainers will bring their Brand of Tough on Confused, along with pistachios and pancakes, to the House and Senate.

That is why we need to vote for Felix for President of the United States! It is time for the White House to become The Grey House! Do not be confused! Feel the Felix Force!

Together we can fight the confused and once and for all be done with all of that ridiculous.

Vote Felix! Vote Parrot Party! Feel the Felix Force!

Day 5 Parrot National Convention
Speakers – Angus Lee LaFollett, VP Candidate
Felix R. LaFollett, accepting the Nomination

Day 5 opened with Angus Lee at the podium, noble and ready, to introduce the candidate of Not Confused.

I am Angus Lee LaFollett, Vice Presidential Candidate.

I am not a parrot.

I am a proud hound of the Catahoula lineage. A dog of the south has no trouble smelling out the best candidate for the 2020 election. My nose, knows.

I welcome you to the last day of the Parrot Party National Convention for 2020!

I told Felix yesterday that I would create a triumphant energized moment for his nomination, and his acceptance speech. I also told him I didn't realize he was serious about all this when I said, yes.

I've known Felix my whole life. Our first day I had just arrived from the rescue, not sure of much, let alone The Confused. Working alongside Felix these 3 years has been an honor. Few are aware of just how Felix handles The Confused. He laughs in it's face.

Do not let his humor fool you. He is super cereal serious about The Confused, it being on his last nerve, and feeling that there is no one else that can handle the level of off-the-chain Confused that permeates our world today.

There is no arguing that today is utterly, emphatically, saturated with confused. Like Kong chew toys with no peanut butter. You want to believe that will be satisfying, but there's something missing. All the good stuff.

And THAT is why I said yes to Felix. He is all the good stuff. I also said yes because he gave me his lunch. And I didn't think he was serious.

He is all the good stuff though, and we need to fix The Confused that has grown from a field of other guys that have taken all the good stuff and replaced it with all not the good stuff. Mostly fake stuff. Stuff I'm not chewing on. I'm not eating chicken treats from other countries.

Listing all the things that are wrong wastes valuable time better spent napping, draping on couches, or better, chasing squirrels. The wrong is The Confused. The fix for The Confused, is The Felix.

He comes ready to start on the first day! He comes fully armed with Trainers ready to cut to the chase and lunch. Removing what's wrong. Replacing them with all the good stuff! They will fill all our Kongs with peanut butters!

Universal Confused Care! All will be covered so none can be infected! And if you have a pre-existing confused, you are covered! Pick your own Doctor of Confused! Feel confident in your treatments of The Confused!

Goats4Votes! Felix offers two goats for laughs. Laughs leave no room for The Confused. He has already had a Goats4Votes App created for applying for your goats! The Grand Union of Goats is ready to deliver the day you apply. When elected President, you'll be able to download the app on day one!

The government website will have a new address! *.grey*

Everything that ever happened in the government before will be released on the FelixAdministration.grey website.

The Confused grows where things aren't known.

For instance;

1. Yes, there are aliens. Aliens are more a people problem than a dog problem. As long as someone opens the door so I can get that squirrel, I'm good.
2. Yes, the space station has been visited by aliens and they can't find the oxygen leak either.
3. Yes, Felix does have a Planet named after him.
4. No, the aliens haven't visited because he's not there.
5. Yes, when aliens hear about Space Force they LOL.

All the good stuffs and more will be at the .grey site.

Felix brings the things that remove The Confused that leave more room for MORE OF THE GOOD THINGS.

You see where he's going. He knows where you think you are going! Today on behalf of the Parrot National Party I nominate Felix Robert LaFollett as Parrot Party Presidential Candidate for the 2020 election year!

And I turn over this auspicious moment and podium to that bird. That Trainer that gives his all until lunch …

…there's squirrels flipping me off outside. I gotta go …

September 4th Parrot National Convention
Felix Robert LaFollett Nomination Acceptance Speech

(Insert ROARING CROWDS OF ROARS AND CHEERS!)

Thank you! Thank you trainees! Thank you for my supports!

(Insert chants of FELIX FELIX FELIX FELIX!)

THANK YOU! Oh yes, thank you! You are right though.

(Insert yells of SPEECH SPEECH SPEECH!!)

Thank you Trainees, Constituents, honored guests, Speakers, and alsotoo, every thebody else! GREY STRENGTH TO YOU!

(Insert yellings of the YAYS! and HIPPO RAYS!!)

I accept the Parrot Party Nomination and am ready to fight The Confused with you!

(Insert the oooooos and ahhhhhhs and excitable joy hollers!)

Since last time I ran for the Presidentialing I have been working on setting the ups and answers for the 2020 election.

As you know, I know where you think you are going, and I already knew we would end up here. The explosionings of The Confused was inevitabled. And I am READY. I am ABLED. I am THE FELIX!

(Insert screamings of the joys and fainting trainees)

Lets cut to the chasers and the brass tackers. On the day ONE, The Felix Administrationings will be ready!

First! My administration will fix the mailsman problem! I can't mail pens and tracking devices fast. YOU can't get treats for your feets fast.

I will fix this by appointing A serious Cockatoo as the Post Master Generator! That other guy is caked in The Confused obviouslies. Cockatoos do not mess around. They do not take the no for the answers. And once they make up their minds to do something...get out of the Tooway.

(Insert cheers of the joys and chants of FIX THAT THINGY!)

Secondlies! I will help the Senegal Senate and Conure Cockatiel House of the Representers pass the Universal Confused Care Act! Enough with the confused acts and amendmentors that get nothing done. The UCCA will provide Confused Care to all who ask, and pre-existing Confused will be covered!

Additionialies! If you are Confused, you get help. If you might be confused, you get help. If you don't want to get confused, you get help! Further the mortars, the UCCA will provide Confused Tests for every theone, every thewhere, no matter the what! These tests will tell you right away if you are confused. Each test will come with a Trainer. They will let you know right away what your problem is.

I am excitables to tell you these tests do not have to be stuck up your nosehole!

(Insert chants of NO MORE NOSEHOLE POKES!!!)

Threelies! Goats4Votes! The Get your Goats4Voting app is ready to be released the day I am elected Presidential. Your Get Your Goats4Voting app will allow you to apply for your goats AND request a Confused test. The Grand Union of Goats has counted all their members and are ready to deliver to you laughs and goats upon receiving your applicationing!

(insert yells and the chants of GOATS GOATS GOATS!!)

Fourthlies! I have conversationed with all the pellet producers of our great country and they have said if I am elected Presidentailing, they will STOP MIXING UP THE COLORS! They have agreed to liberate the colors for our choices! No more High (insert dreaded color here) Pellet Ratios again!

It was pretty the simple really. I found out three pellet people didn't have Trainers. So I sent three Emergency Trainers to their locations to straighten out their red wagons of confused. The Felix Administration will not waste timers, we will always get the thingys done!

(Insert joyouslies of the yells of HURRAYS!! FELIX FELIX!!)

The Felix Administration has all the Trainers ready to GO! the day we know I win! Once the week I will appear on FelixTV to tell you what is going on so you know what is not getting confused.

I will put the Air Force One airplane away during my administrationings. We all know now ZOOM is the way to say HEY! I am not wasting the times or the money running arounds to talk to leaders when we can just sit down and ZOOM chat.

I like ZOOM chat. I did it once and my Felix Face Box turned green when I talked. You can make it stay green if you talk a lot. In the case you were wondering about that.

I will alsotoo, not be messing around with messing around with parties and feeding leaders from far away. There is no time for all that messing around. I have the four years to fix The Confused and then I am going on the vacation to my retirement condo.

And now the campaignings begin!

Pay the attentions so you know what you need to know and what you don't need to waste your time knowing so you can spend that time making treats for your Trainer!

I will, alsotoo, announce the winners of the Parrot National Conventioning Contest of Supports on Monday. There are so many supports out there to appreciate! Thank you for all of that! I will announce new exiting campaignery thingys!

The Felix New Flavor of Presidentialing Perfection Campaign Trail Mix! New tracking devices! Presidentialing Pens!
I accept this nomination. And now The Felix Presidentialing Campaign really starts. But first I need before lunch snacks.

And a digesting nap.

Thank you for my supports! Thank you for votes! Thank you alsotoo for knowing The Felix is the FIX for Confused!
Grey Strength!

Get your tracking devices! Get synced to the Felix Fire!
https://www.cafepress.com/imwithfelix

September 8th, 2020

The weirdo is growing like weirdo weeds. We are now surrounded by all kinds of weirdo. So much weirdo. Mom says she is on her last nerve endings about all of "it". I have the no ideas about what "it" is, but I am pretty sure it better not walk up to her and say hi.

I am pretty the sure she will punch it in the face.

Mom is looking less confused and more rager. I hope she doesn't explode. She looks like she could explode. A trainee can only handle so much, which is why a trainee needs a Trainer.

Trainees say, "Hey Felix, why should I want a parrot any theway?"

"That question proves you are confused. Get one immediatlies."

"But Felix, I'm fine."

"No, you are not."

These conversationals don't last long.

That is why I am just finishing up my book, "*Dear Felix Diary Thingy; Felix in the Time of Confused*". I'm excitables about this new answer to confused questionings.

Mom says she is in the last Ed it. I have no idea who Ed is. What he has to do with The Felix and The Felix Book is beyond me. Alsotoo, mom says that Ed it, is not the other "it" on her last nerve endings.

So I am here thinking, "Well, how many ITS do you have any theway!?"

Mom has issues of its.

Great news though any theway!

The new Felix Campaign Trail Mix "Presidentialing Perfection" is availables now AND a Presidentialing Pen is in every bag. Which is super cereal impressive. You can write a speech.

Or make a shopping list for your Trainer with that pen. Alsotoo, PENS!!! That is right! Pens if you don't want Trail Mix flavors you can just get the pen and start making the essentialing list of snack attack shopping for your Trainer. It's win and winner chicken ate the dinner!

I have told mom the constituent supports is SO impressives that there has to be 15 winners of the supporting contest. So, I am working on adding the other 5 before I tell everyone the win winner chicken ate the dinner list of winners! Of the course, every winner gets a full set of campaign buttons of tracking AND a presidentialing pen.

Getting all these excitables done while mom is itching her its is not easy. But that is what a Presidential does to fix The Confused. You just have to not give the its. And I do not.

Dogheads killed another mom screamer bug this morning. I saw it crawling across the floor coughing.

"Hey screamer bug, you don't look so good."

COUGH "Ya, I think it's something I ate."

"Was it yellow? Cause I almost die every time I eat one of those."

And before screamer bug could answer me, doghead snorfled it's butt, mom screamed and stomped it, and then ran into the wall.

It's going to be one of those weeks.

September 9th, 2020

Angus Doghead decided there was a evil doer doing something outside. Dante Doghead said, "WHAT?"

"EVIL DOER!"

Dante ran after Angus, arounding the corner, and ran into a wall just like mom. "What's he doing?"

Angus ran before Dante, arounding that corner, and ran into that wall just like mom, alsotoo. "EVIL! He's doing EVIL!"

Angus tried to get off Dante, and Dante tried to push Angus off to get off him. And then they slipped and fell into the wall again. Mom's last nerve endings stuck out like those screamer bug antennas.

"STOP!"

Angus and Dante used each other for the ladder and ran around mom to the front window. Barking at the same time but not saying the same things at all.

"EVIL DOER!"
"WHAT'S HE DOING!?"
"EVIL!!"

"Dante Angus Stop! There's nothing there!"

Then Angus and Dante jumped up and down and they looked ridiculous jumping. They have scrawny legs and goofer feets. Dante was dancing and wiggly his butt rope jumping and Angus was hopping and the hairs on his butt rope made it look like he stole it from a porcupine. And now THAT porcupine doesn't have a tail and he looks like a hamster.

"Dante down! Angus down!" Mom's last nervings fell off. "EVERY BODY IN A BOX!"

Yup, they fell right off onto the floor. Which ironicallies had a screamer bug crawling across it because he was dying because he obviouslies ate something yellow.

I know his pains.

Mom screamed. Dante jumped on mom and she fell into another wall. Angus barked out the window at nothing again and hopped like a rabbit with a porcupine tail. Then Dante snorfled the screamer bug butt and mom found another nerve ending. She pushed Dante off the bug butt.

"Do not snorfle that bug, Dante. He ate poison!"

AND THAT is when I knew for the facts that yellow pellets are poison.

You would think dogheads would end up in boxes with breads and water for three weeks. But no, no they get the cookies Aunt Christine made for them. And she sent a cookie kit with the cooked cookies. Because she knew mom doesn't cook right. I am also sure she was trying to protect The Felix from the house fire.

Which I have to ask her right the now; Why did you send a kit not cooked when you know she starts fires and makes panslurpies? Was this a joke? Are you trying to TRAIN mom? That's my job.

Alsotoo, dogheads love these cookies so much when mom says stop, with a cookie, no one falls into walls.

This is amaziballs!

Additionalies, I took the tastes of the try outs and these are delicious! I have the other question for Aunt Christine, why don't you have Felix shaped cookie cutters in that bag? Hmm? I think it would be a good business decisioning to do that.

I am recommending these cookies right now, alsotoo, if you cook like mom, I recommend building a fire escape first. And wear a fire alarm on a necklace.

If you cook like dad. Never themind. You can use your pancake spatula for this recipe. It fits.

Unlike Dante's butt rope in my nosehole. Which I just now learned. Against my will and opinion.

https://christineschopshop.com

September 10th, 2020

This morning was the FeLOL! I fooled mom and she thought it was Dante Doghead and it was me. Doghead whines are so easy to do, I don't even have to try! Dante Doghead whines are the easiest to do ever! FeLOLing.

So I started whining. And mom say, "Dante, shhh it's too early."

I am cracking the ups in my bed. She thinks I'm a Doghead.

Dante Doghead dreaming whine

"Dante baby, it's okay. It's just a dream." Then mom rolls over in her bed. I hear her fight her pillows. She looses the fight. I hate to say this out the louds Diary, but I'm pretty the sure she dream drools on her pillows. But any theway, I am cracking the ups in my bed.

Dante Doghead whine ruff dream running feets

"Dante baby. Honey shhh, it's okay it's not time to ..." And then she fell asleep! FeLOLING!

I am cracking the ups in my bed. She can't even think it's Dante, she is so drooler sleepy.

Dante Doghead chasing a squirrel in the sleeps and barks

"It's okay D ...is kay..." Mom is desleeperious! FeLOLing!!!

Dante Doghead whine of let me up on the bed with you whining

"Okay Dante, hang on." Then she is awake and rolling the over and I am FeLOLing! And she starts petting the doghead, (I would never touch a doghead head. You don't really know where that thingy has been). I am so FeLOLing! I am watching through my Felix Hole of the Observationings. And cracking the ups.

"Hey, wait a minute. You're asleep ..."

I am so cracking the ups.

Then mom looks through The Felix Hole of the Observationings and sees me FeLOLing.

fartsound *George Bush chuckle*

She left me no choice.

Epiloguer
By The Felix

Well, I suppose this is just as the good of the place to stop as any of the other places to stop.

When mom said she wanted to make the Felix Diary Thingy a book I was skepticaled. Mostly because she thought about this alone. Alsotoo, there is no end to a diary to say "the end".

Unless of the course if I die of the low blood sugars. Which I almost did after breakfast yesterday before lunch.

Mom is still training unsuccessfullies. Her confused is terminal. Dad did not make the pancakes today, but today is Thursday and not SaturDADday.

The Dactyls are taking naps right now only because dad is mowing his grasses and mom is writing words and dogheads are asleep. For a dactyl, that's not inspirational for the exciteables.

If I don't win the Presidentialing Campaign I am going to take the vacation. Probables for the few days and then I will work on The Confused around here. Which is mom.

No matter the what, always work on The Confused that's close to you. Let's be the honest. Any thebody can fix confused. If they want to, and any thebody can ask another body to help. And then you have two bodies working to fix confused.

You know where I'm going here.
And I know where you think you are going.

Made in the USA
Middletown, DE
14 December 2020